Business Essentials for Writers

How to make money in an ever-changing industry

James P. Nettles

Author Essentials Publications
Charlotte, NC

James P. Nettles. Writer's Guide to Business
Author Essentials Publications, Charlotte, NC
First Edition, V1.0
Cover Art by: Melissa McArthur, Clicking Keys Editing
Edited by: Melissa McArthur, Clicking Keys Editing
https://clickingkeys.com
& Theresa Glover

For Sophie.

Table of Contents

Acknowledgements

I have a plethora of people to thank for both directly and indirectly contributing to this, and let me say, for all the good stuff it's thanks to their influence, and if there's something you don't like, it's all on me.

For Gail Z. Martin, thanks for the many years of mentorship and road trips, John Hartness for the long discussions and helping keep focus, and to Theresa and Melissa for having pounded this scramble of essays, topics and errant commas into a coherent form.

Not to mention everyone who has helped to beta read, ask and answer questions, provide feedback, and sometimes just give me the look that asks if I really meant to put that in, Darin, Rick, Ken, Venessa, Ben, Andi, Nancy, Jeanne, Melisa, Jason, Joelle, Jay, Robyne, Charity, Nicole, Kyle, Kindra, Edd and so many other authors I've sat down and talked with over the years.

For my parents who taught me both love for language and the fundamentals of being an entrepreneur.

And Adrianne, who keeps trying to keep me honest.

Welcome

"A book is made from a tree. It is an assemblage of flat, flexible parts (still called "leaves") imprinted with dark pigmented squiggles. One glance at it and you hear the voice of another person, perhaps someone dead for thousands of years. Across the millennia, the author is speaking, clearly and silently, inside your head, directly to you. Writing is perhaps the greatest of human inventions, binding together people, citizens of distant epochs, who never knew one another. Books break the shackles of time--proof that humans can work magic."

— *Carl Sagan*

If you've picked this book up, it means you are ready to move to the next phase in your career and make your creative pursuit profitable. Maybe you've been doing it a while and are trying to figure out why things aren't working. Maybe you've even been at it for years and are looking for the next edge. Or maybe you are taking your first fledgling steps. Depending on where you are in your career, you will find different levels of value and understanding from this text.

The business of writing has changed a great deal since my first forays into it in the 1980s. I started on the journalism path, and did some short stories, but mostly worked for clients. As I moved into my career, I did a great deal of business planning, project planning, and research. Today I do a mix of fiction and non-fiction writing, consulting in the business, working with speakers and presenters, and other consulting for corporate and entrepreneurial clients.

If you are just starting out, or just want to get an idea how the business works, you will get a good overview of the business and the industry. If you are an experienced and published author, editor, or in any other part of the industry, you should find ideas and resources on ways to improve yourself and your business.

This book, and the program it is a part of, results from distilling down a lot of information to the most basic concepts. I developed it as a combination of business fundamentals with all the rest of the pieces on how to manage your product, your business, and essentially your life balance as a content creator.

I'll leave your creative outlets and products up to you.

I created this project because I was raised in business, I've worked it, consulted for a lot of clients in my life, and found myself helping my friends more and more. Writers, painters, jewelers, sculptors, iron workers and more were having the same fundamental problems as my entrepreneurial and corporate clients. They wanted to know how to produce more work, and then how to sell it. Yeah, I said it. It's okay to make money from your creative outlets. I'll dig into it deeper later, but the idea of having to be a starving artist to be creative is bull.

The digital revolution has touched all of our lives, and I've had the good fortune to be part of it. Like so many other industries, writing and publishing has undergone a transformation.

I remember seeing the first e-reader in the early 2000s. At the time I traveled forty-eight weeks a year for business and consumed two or three books a week or more. The idea of an electronic book had its appeal, but battery life and the limited number of books available kept me from making the jump. Not to mention, I am one of those that loves the experience of holding it in my hands, and the smell of the paper. Even now, some authors I must have in hardback, or at least paperback to fully enjoy the experience. Even so, the majority of my purchases are ebooks.

I think this reflects the overall change in the market, but the other side of the digital revolution has been the changes it's led to in the writing and publishing fields. Today, anyone can become a published author. The downside? Anyone can become a published author today.

In the past, while it was and still is painful to have Publishers as gatekeepers, it also implies a certain level of style and quality depending on the publishing house. For a time, a mass influx of mixed quality self-published books hit the market. Now the rest of the business engine is catching up to provide publisher level services, and providers such as Amazon, Barnes and Noble and Kobo are doing more to ensure some level of quality and service, but the responsibility lies with the author.

I started this book out of a series of blog posts and social media commentaries replying to questions and issues friends and clients had, mistakes we'd made and our victories. As I'd ask questions and we'd talk about key aspects of the business side, on many topics even experienced professional authors often would give me a blank stare. Others told me about how they run their careers to varying degrees of success.

Being who I am, I shared my view that having a career as a writer was more than just that, a career. If you're a writer, an editor, or one of the many other roles in the publishing industry, and unless you produce content for a given company, you either own or are a major part of a microbusiness. You may also hear the word Solopreneur.

Being a business owner requires a different mindset than someone who has a career in a given field, working for others. We all work for someone, and hopefully it's our customers. This is a scary thought for most people. Most artists just want to create. To be successful though, you've got to understand all of the other pieces, and how the puzzle fits together.

I hope you find this book entertaining given some of the dryer topics. More importantly, though I can't solve all of your problems and answer all of your questions, I hope it helps you grow and develop your career as a writer, publisher, editor, artist, or the myriad of others who are part of this creative and vital industry, and find the answers that you need.

I'm not going to cover any of this to an exhaustive level because each one of these topics could be its own book. Some can be their own libraries. This program is designed to give you the basics so you know what you need to know and have the context for your next step.

I'm here for you.

In my career so far, I've done a lot of years in implementing technology projects, some huge, some small, but I've done a lot of them. I've worked for Fortune 100's and mom-and-pop's operations. I've also owned businesses, consulted for others. I even started my life as an accountant.

Impressed?

I only tell you this to give you a little bit of perspective on where I'm coming from. It just means I've been given plenty of chances to make mistakes and learn from them. And I'm going to share that with you so you can make your own, *different* ones. You will begin to think not only creatively but carry that creativity into learning how to be a business owner.

Business is a rational way of thinking and acting.

Being creative is a passionate way of life and being.

For many, it is finding the balance between the two that determines success, or failure for both themselves personally, and their business. And if you keep reading, I'm going to be your best friend, your business coach, your counselor, and sometimes the heartless bastard that gives you a kick in the ass that no one else will. But I'll do it with love.

Mostly.

- Jim

Introduction

It's Your Circus, It's Your Monkeys

"We need to have a beginner's mind to think about what's happening."
-Marc Benioff

As a creator, it may scare you to think of yourself as a business, a business owner, and a brand. If your business is in publishing, or any of the support businesses in the industry, you should already have this in mind to some extent.

Creative endeavors operate somewhat differently from other commercial enterprises. The work tends to be out of desire and passion as much as a job. The hard part can be remembering to keep all the parts moving, not just the pieces that drive you.

To give a little perspective on the various facets of business, and all of the roles that are part of it, we're going to pretend you're a different kind of entertainer. Channel your inner P. T. Barnum.

Your business is a small traveling circus that does themed shows based on classical fantasy stories such as the writings of J.R.R. Tolkien and CS Lewis (and being an author is definitely a circus).

In keeping with the theme, your current show is named "Master of the One Ring," and your logo is a golden ring surrounded by animals and performers in costume. You, as the ringmaster wear a wizard's outfit and have a catchy theme song. have snippets of video from your show on YouTube and your website. This is all part of your branding.

You run ads on Facebook, attend some local events, and travel ahead of the show and put up signs and billboards around town announcing, "Master of the Ring Circus, Saturday and Sunday!" That's advertising.

Imagine on Friday, you parade through town to the convention center where you'll be appearing, and a pair of chimpanzees carry the "Master of the Ring Circus" banner at the front of the performers. You hand out some free plastic rings to all of the kids along the way. You get the observers to all do Facebook Lives and IG Stories along the way, and offer discounts if they tag you. That's promotion.

Along the route, the monkeys see the pink flamingos in the mayor's front yard, and decide to steal them all to decorate his big oak tree with them. The local paper (along with everyone else in sight) snaps a picture of the mayor clutching his head and staring up into the tree. That's publicity.

When you, as the ringmaster, step up to the mayor, and share a laugh about what your barrel of monkeys has done, and maybe give his eminence a few free tickets, you have moved into public relations.

When everyone in town lines up at the ticket booth, buying programs and t-shirts, that's the magic ring of sales!

And if you planned, scripted, trained, rehearsed and arranged the whole thing? From branding to sales, this whole process is called marketing.

But there is a whole lot more to being a business owner.

Coming up with new products and new shows is product research and development.

Scripting, rehearsing, and refining your product, and bringing it to market is production.

Ordering all of the t-shirts, plastic rings, posters and everything else you sell is inventory management and purchasing.

Keeping track of your schedule, booking locations, mapping out your path is logistics.

Budgeting, tracking the money coming in and going out, and the rest of the financial stuff is accounting.

Everything else from keeping the wheels on the bus to booking performers is operations.

We will touch on all of these topics and more in this book When some of it feels a little dense or dry, picture a monkey flinging it at you. The most important lesson to come out of this whole book, as the owner and operator of a small business, as well as the creative genius, remember one thing; *it's your circus, and it's your monkeys*.

The Starving Artist Lie

"Over the last forty years, many educators, decision-makers, and even some parents have come to regard the arts as peripheral, and let's face it, frivolous—especially the visual arts, with their connotation of" the starving artist" and the mistaken concept of necessary talent."

— *Betty Edwards, The New Drawing on the Right Side of the Brain*

Over the years, I have been in conversations with a lot of creative people. When we talked about the business side of their art, there was a feeling of guilt for charging any material amount for their work. Some did not recognize the value in it and believed no one would pay for it. Some even told me they believed receiving compensation for their work cheapened it or would take away its value. Some even believe their financial struggles were the foundation for their creativity.

This is the myth of the "starving artist."

And it angers me to no end, and is one of the drivers for me to develop this book.

Throughout time, development of the arts has been a sign of an advanced culture. You usually don't have time to paint if you are worried about where your next meal is coming from, or if the barbarians are at the gates. Even so, people created art in caves 40,000 years ago. We have maintained our stories and histories through oral tradition. Art is at the core of our souls as a species.

Art has been so valued, the wealthy and powerful of many cultures have embraced the patronage system. By supporting creative work, patrons raised their political and social stature by the number and reputation of the artists they sponsored, and the quality of their work. During the Renaissance, artists were so valued they often lived in luxury on the estates of their patrons.

It was understood that creativity flourished when the artist has the freedom to follow their passions.

What happened?

I theorize it started in the sixteenth century with the Reformation. People were encouraged to live simply and believed in hard work as a reward in itself. In Protestant regions, countless pieces of iconography and other art were destroyed *en masse*. The volume of art produced dropped drastically. Styles tended to be simpler and more utilitarian in what little was produced. Creative outlets, especially the arts, were often seen as wasteful and taking resources away from the productive use of time.

Moving forward into the modern day, we still see many artists and consumers both devalue their work. We face:

Internal myths (our own beliefs)

- Believing our own work has little or no value - asking ourselves, why would anyone be interested in my work?

- Imposter syndrome. Your knowledge, experience, and perspective is unique. Don't let anyone take that from you. We compare ourselves to others and invest them with the power we have within us. Our (false) belief that our work isn't good enough for someone to buy.
- Thinking there is no market for our style of work.
- Feeling it's wrong to charge for art, that it should be free to everyone.
- Feeling uncomfortable or wrong marketing and advertising our work, or that commercialization takes away some of its uniqueness.
- The belief that "my work is too unique, too special to be shared."

External myths (societal beliefs and pressures)
- Being an artist, a writer, or other creator isn't a "real job."
- Art is a gift, meant to be shared. Friends and family especially can take advantage and not recognize the blood, sweat and tears poured into your work.
- Creative work has little or no real value, unless a brand is attached. Large scale commercial work replaces unique and individual pieces.
- In the age of the big box store and the digital revolution, intellectual property should all be free.

Have you heard someone say, "It's just words on a page" or "It's just beads on a string." We all have heard, "Oh, I can do that."

Invite people to try. In many cases, they could do something creative. They just don't. And even if they do, it still won't be exactly your style, your skill, or your final product.

For those that start this journey, we all have our inspirations and teachers. I believe every one of us has something creative to share with the world.

They are still myths, no lies we tell ourselves, and you can succeed around them. Here's the good news.
- Creating something unique and of quality has great value. Never let anyone tell you otherwise. People will pay for it, when you find your market.
- Your detractors are right, on one point. Creating is not a "real job." It's so much more. That's the point of this book. It's a profession. It means owning a business, and being responsible for your own destiny. It's the people content to live in their "real jobs" and go home to be entertained that don't understand the reality of the work.
- Your biggest detractors and least supportive people may be that way either because of their own fears to take risks, or jealousy that you are. That's their problem, not yours.

- Yes, you need to understand your markets, and your competition, but not to compare your successes or failures. Understand and study how they have succeeded. Most people are happy to build productive relationships, if you ask. Remember, it's a two-way street.
- It is not a sin to be paid fairly for your work. Money is simply a tool we all need. Your time, and the output of your skills and effort has value.
- It takes an investment of time and money to build your skills, create a finished product, bring it to market, and sell it. You are entitled to recoup your investment and prosper from it.

Andy Warhol said, "Being good in business is the most fascinating kind of art. Making money is art and working is art and good business is the best art."

Forget the starving artist. Be the thriving artist.

Is Your Business Taking You for a Ride?

"A successful man is one who can lay a firm foundation with the bricks others have thrown at him."
- David Brinkley

I met David Brinkley when I was in college. I covered a speech he was giving for the University of South Carolina (the same way I got to meet many people and be exposed to a lot of ideas), and while I don't remember a lot from his speech, I do remember the tone and confidence in his voice as he remembered some of the challenges he had faced earlier in his career. The part I do remember was him talking about building a solid foundation for yourself, your life, and your career.

At the time, I also volunteered in the Small Business Center at USC, and did work with people who were trying to start their own small businesses, from coffee shops to copy shops, and mostly other retail type work or micro manufacturing. Even today, I know a lot of business owners, and the question comes up, "what is a business?"

Most people will say, "I write books," "I create art," or "I develop games." These are not businesses. These are products and services. Any business, every business, whether an author cranking out books or a multinational manufacturing conglomerate is the same thing. The business is nothing more than the people, framework, and processes that allow you to move forward and accomplish your goals. In other words, a business is nothing more than the engine that takes in time and resources and generates money. The question is; how efficiently does your engine run, and does it give you more of a return than what you put into it?

As an author, it is difficult, nigh impossible to separate yourself from your business. But remember, you are not your business. Your business in the publishing world is to help bring the written word to a given audience. Your job in the business is to make sure someone is wearing the needed hats, even if it is all just you. But you still need to remember, your business is a separate, living, breathing organism. One that exists to serve you and your interests, not the other way around.

From a 101 perspective, there are really only five parts to any business. Think about it like a riding a bicycle.

You'll find there are many different types of rides, for every purpose and every budget. Your ten speed probably will not survive a hard mountain trail. Not every business model serves every business.

This book, and the program it is a part of, is based on the structure of a business, with each chapter and topic designed to help you develop your business plan to have a model to follow, and in such a way that you can see and focus on each of these factors and develop a sustainable business in the publishing industry. By working through each section of the plan, we address not only the plan, but actions to take, and the approaches and attitudes to use to be successful, and general business practices.

I know this may look a little daunting, but we're going to break all of this into pieces and come at it from a few directions. If we think about business structure like a bicycle, there are with five core areas of business:

1. The People are the core not only of any business, but of society as a whole. We ride together. Without other people, not only can we not make and deliver good work, but we have no one to buy it from us. This would be not only our authors, editors, and artists, but also agents, publicists, accountants, bookstore staff, and of course our readers. Every person involved in the journey of any given product from the person with an idea to the one who buys it depends on the wheels turning. With the people component, what you really need to understand is not only their mindset, but yours as well. Thought dictate action.

   As the CEO, you are the most important person and your Mindset is the core of your business. It gives us vision, creativity, drive, and keeps us going when we don't think we can. The good news is that if the worst happens and we have built a solid foundation, you have a place to start from. If we expect the best, the more likely we are to get it. Buckle on your helmet, and keep it safe.

2. The Foundation is a lot like the frame. Everything attaches to the frame in some way or another, and it has to be able to support everything it carries to get us from one place to another, but it can't take us anywhere on its own.

a. The core of the Foundation is the vision that the founders and leaders hold for the business to give it purpose, and the customers it looks to serve.

b. The strength of the business comes from the knowledge, skills, and drive to see the business succeed.

c. The architecture defines the processes and methodologies used by the business.

d. A solidly constructed Foundation can be used over and over again, only needing tweaks and modifications to deliver new and different products and services to your end customer instead of having to start from scratch.

3. Sales and Marketing are like the bells, whistles and lights or trading cards you put in the spokes to announce your presence, and even the paint and racing stripes to "give you speed" and make you look good. Maybe it is the flowery basket on the front. It is any way you are making potential customers aware of you, your work, and your products, and to communicate who you and your brand are. It is how you connect with your readers to find what they want from you. It is every way in which you interact with them be it in person, social media, or your website.

4. Technology and Operations are the wheels on your bike. They are what keep you rolling uphill and downhill. They represent a fundamental and revolutionary technology which encompasses everything about delivering a final product to your customer. It is scheduling an appointment with your editor to review your latest book, sitting at a convention to network or sell books to publishers, it is uploading your manuscript and cover to Amazon. If the wheels aren't turning, your business isn't going anywhere. Occasionally, you need to be ready to change a flat tire.

5. Finance and Accounting are the handles, chains, pedals, and brakes that turn your effort into results. We have to pour our resources in to get energy out and use those tools to steer. Ultimately, making money is the goal of any business, and differentiates a business from a hobby.

When you first start to ride, you have to learn balance, how to lean into a turn, how to pedal uphill and coast downhill. You have accidents. You fall over. You have to learn how to stop. Business is no different.

Another hard lesson is learning to control the bicycle. The biggest mistake I see entrepreneurs make is that they create themselves a job, but do not see themselves as business owners, or CEOs. When you have a job, someone else is giving direction, and at the end of the day, you leave the job and go home. You can always get another job somewhere else. Owning a business is like raising a child. It means continuous care, feeding, and attention, until it's big enough to take care of itself for periods of time, or you have trusted people that carry some of the responsibility. Once you put that kid on a bike, you cannot always control where it goes, but at the same time, you can get a lot from the ride.

It is worth noting, many of the topics will touch more than one of these areas and know that People are a part of every step of the way.

As you progress through the book, we tackle each of these sections with four focuses:

1. Mindset is the attitude and confidence to use your intelligence, talents and skills to meet your goals.

2. Strategy is a vision, creating a plan, and working towards your long-term goals.
3. Tactical Actions are the steps you take at (hopefully) the right place and the right time to execute your strategy.
4. Operational Actions are the day to day and regular routines of business, linking your strategic plan to your Tactical Actions.

Think of this book like the training wheels and helmet. Even after you have been riding for years, you still sometimes will crash, often through events outside of your control.

You may have noticed the one thing I did not mention. Your product. Your book. Your ebook. The audiobook. TV and movie rights. Merchandizing rights. Services. Appearances. Voice work. Sketching Deadpool as a pledge in Animal House.

A properly structured business, even if you're the only staff, allows you to develop different goods for sale. If you are going to have a run for the long term, you will need it, and building a model that can change and grow with you. Sometimes you have to replace tires and rims. Sooner or later, it's time to upgrade.

If you don't take anything else away from reading this book, here's the most important lesson I've ever been taught: get rid of the idea that you can't fail if you don't try. It's the exact opposite. If you don't try, you can never succeed. Stretch your boundaries, and leap past that comfort zone. Keep the first aid kit handy for the many bumps and bruises along the way and keep on going.

As much as I'd like for this to be a one stop manual on business, it's going to be just one resource and guide in your journey. It's meant to be a first step to give you the basics and tell you what you do not know; not to turn you into a master. That will take a little more time.

1: People

The Most Important Person in Your Business

"The present is theirs; the future, for which I really worked, is mine."
- Nikola Tesla

When you consider the most important person in any business, it's the one who has the vision and gives direction. As an author, that's you.

I cannot reinforce enough the idea that being an author means owning a business. The biggest mistake that most entrepreneurs make is underestimating the amount of work and resources it will take to be successful, and that it's not a straight line. Even the most successful entrepreneurs in any business have ridden a roller coaster of failure and success.

Sometimes, it's a matter of how you define success that's most important, and to keep going when the days are hardest.

I've found that most entrepreneurial people are also creatively driven, but many creative people have issues with, or fear and detest the business side of the equation. One of the best examples is between Tesla and Edison. I've long studied both men, their inventive and creative approaches, and how they tackled the business side as well.

Nikola Tesla was a brilliant man. A futurist, inventor, engineer, and a true visionary in terms of what could be done. Even in designing death rays and earthquake machines, I believe it was as much a pursuit of knowledge and benefit to his fellow man as anything. He was driven to learn, understand, and experiment on the world around us, often by himself, or at most with small teams of assistants.

Thomas Edison too was a genius in terms of technology and innovation, but the man knew how to run a business, and was a genius at marketing. He formed and grew a think tank and experimental lab, employing scientists, engineers, and innovative minds. Most of Edison's patents were really the inventions of his people.

If these two men had been able to team up creatively, I firmly believe we'd live in a much different world. Unfortunately, they became diametrically opposed and despised each other. This conflict may have spurred both men further separately than they could have done together.

What does this have to do with writing, or being an author? Nothing directly.

I mention them, because I believe there's value in studying each of them and their approaches to creative endeavors. I'm not suggesting modeling yourself on either man, but they make a great case study for business in the creative and innovative world.

At one point, Tesla was one of the many engineers working for Edison. Famously, Edison offered Tesla $50,000 if he could fix the direct current motor in time to be delivered for a contract. Tesla dove into the project with abandon, and increased the efficiency of the motor, ultimately saving the contract and making Edison a fortune. Edison then backed out of paying Tesla what was promised, creating the great rift between the two [telling Tesla he did not understand American humor to get out of the verbal agreement instead of paying up].

Lesson number one, if it sounds too good to be true, it probably is. And lesson number two, get it in writing.

Despite Edison offering him a substantial raise at the time (from $18 a week to $25), Tesla left to build his own competing startup company.

When we own the business, it's up to us to make it work. Tesla started out digging ditches and doing manual labor until he could get enough investors and capital to get his company off the ground.

Tesla mainly operated as an experimental lab and developed major innovations in electrical power. In the infamous "Power Wars" or the "War of the Currents" of the late 1880's into the 1890's, Edison, backed by JP Morgan held fast to direct current model, which Tesla radically improved in efficiency. Tesla developed and patented the revolutionary alternating current technology, backed by George Westinghouse (which is the backbone of the modern world).

And, thus, was born AC/DC (and the inspiration for a band of the ages).

The battle raged between the two, with Edison fighting the propaganda war and Tesla trying to live with science and fact on his side. Edison invented the electric chair as a means of execution as a means of proving how unsafe AC was as a technology. He even sponsored events electrocuting animals as a spectacle, most famously an elephant.

The war culminated at the 1893 World's Fair, and the City of Light.

Using Edison's direct current, General Electric put in a bid of one million dollars (you know you're hearing that in Doctor Evil's voice) to power and illuminate the event. After negotiation, they dropped the price tag to a mere $554,000 and got ready to move forward.

Unknown to them at the time, George Westinghouse using Tesla's AC technology, put in a bid of $399,000 and won the job. This ultimately launched our move as a country into the age of alternating current.

I can hear you now. All of this is quite interesting, but I'm a writer. Or an editor. Why do I care?

We're talking about the stuff powering the laptop or tablet in front of you, or printed the physical book is Direct Current (Edison's power) converted to Alternating Current (Tesla's juice.) It is also the difference between business and creativity and finding that balance.

In the end, Edison rued the soured relationship with Tesla and appreciated his genius. Edison died a wealthy man.

Tesla sold his patents for AC for only a couple of thousand dollars, as he believed in the benefit it could bring for mankind. Some years later, Westinghouse pulled his patronage of Tesla due to fears over free energy, and the wireless transmission of power. Though he worked on projects until the day he died, Tesla, despite his genius and everything he'd done, was penniless and living on the generosity of friends.

My point for you is simple. Lesson number three. Know the value of your work, and never be afraid or embarrassed to get paid for what it's worth.

As an author, you're probably not going to revolutionize everyday life, but one could argue Jack Canfield, E. A. Poe, J.K Rowling, J.R.R. Tolkien, Gene Roddenberry, George Lucas and Arthur C. Clarke among others have definitely had their influence.

Times change, and so do people's tastes and styles.

We currently live in a renaissance period for artisans. People want organic foods, craft beers, farm-to-table restaurants, and hand-crafted but high-quality items. Big chains like the Golden Arches and Wally World are going through major challenges, when not that many years ago, they were corporate juggernauts.

In this environment creative people can thrive. The technology is available for everyone who has the least motivation to bring their stuff to market, whether it's quality or not.

I'll repeat this throughout the book: I'm not the one to inspire your creativity. That's all you. Find your muse and your inspiration. Try new things with reckless abandon. Except skydiving: wear a parachute.

And remember, you and your work have value, but your value as a person is not based on your work.

The People of the Business

"People are the core of every business. Businesses are based on relationships, and relationships are based on people. I would go to an average restaurant run by amazing people over an outstanding restaurant run by awful people."
-Marcus Lemonis

As authors, there is an imperative to understand people. We have to know how to connect and communicate. We need to know how to push reader's intellectual and emotional buttons to get the desired result. What we often miss are the interactions with people right in front of us. Those real, living beings.

The ones that give us the shot at a career.

Many authors can be reserved and introverted. I certainly go through my phases of it. I've got a few friends in the industry who went into writing because they loved the written word and they believed it was a way to simply to avoid people.

If your goal is to build a career while being all but anonymous, in today's world it will likely limit your success. We are no longer in the age of Harper Lee or even Bill Waterston. We depend on others, even if the connections are only through the virtual world. Humans are still fundamentally social creatures, even if we as individuals are not.

In the publication industry, you will have to not only meet and interact with many types of people, and many personalities, but many different functions within the industry as well. This first chapter is dedicated to the roles, responsibilities, and business functions you are likely to interact with in publishing.

As you consider the work you intend to do yourself versus what you hire out, ask yourself. even if you have the skills, do you have the time? Would your efforts be better served elsewhere if someone else can take care of for you?

No matter what, you cannot do it alone.

The people you partner with and that surround you will determine your success. And they can't all be friends. You need people that give you critical and honest feedback, regardless of your feelings. And very few people have all the skills required to run a business from beginning to end.

Your Fans and Customers

The first person you must consider in the publishing business, besides yourself, is your potential or existing customer. Your reader or listener. Your fans. Without readers, your book makes a lovely paperweight. As you develop your craft and your marketing, the better you know and understand your readers, the better you will be able to connect with them.

You may even have a fan base that's never actually read your work by creating iconic stories or characters that resonate with a. larger audience. The act of being popular or known can be enough to bring you new readers and fans; thus, is the world of social media and being "internet famous." Obscurity is our biggest enemy.

Effective authors create work that resonates with the reader, whether it is the newest thriller, or a textbook. By understanding your target reader as an individual, you must know how to better communicate with them, and market to them. From this group, you can develop your hard-core base of "true fans," who are your biggest and best salespeople.

You also understand who your audience is not and can avoid wasting time and resources trying to reach them.

Writers

As a writer, a small part of your business is actually the process of… writing. And I'm not talking about all of the time you spend on FaceTweetOScope "Marketing" yourself.

I am not going to dig into the details of the process of writing, or style, or fixing your manuscript. There are plenty of resources out there to help you do that. I am not talking about how to become a writer. That is easy. Go write, and you are a writer.

I am speaking about the business side of being a freelance writer; being a professional. You may be asking yourself, how do I become a professional? You develop a piece of work and then find someone to compensate you for it. If you have a check in hand after handing over some of your work, you are now a professional. Or at least on your way.

Often the image we have of writers are the person sitting in the coffee shop brooding over their unfinished novel between hashing out cups of ultra-skim-grande-mocha-latte-with-a-half-gainer-and-a-triple-axel as a barista. There are plenty of positions out there that allow you to exercise your skills as a writer, from journalism to copy development to corporate content development. Much of this book can apply to you too, but this book is targeted to people who want to develop professionally as an independent or freelance writer.

What does it mean to be a professional freelancer? Being a professional means knowing, owning, and understanding your business, and treating it like a business as a business owner, not as a job.

If you do work for someone as an employee, such as in media, being a professional means having the integrity to do your best work every day, and make sure tomorrow is better.

Writing Assistants

You can think of writing assistants as apprentices. If you are still building your career, spending time with a more experienced author and trading time for experience and mentorship can be a great trade. For the author, it means an investment of time, but in trade, your assistant can provide an extra set of eyes on your work and handle a lot of smaller daily tasks. It can be invaluable for both parties at events and conventions.

Editors

Editors are the life blood and safety net for writers. Though all writers do varying degrees of editing (or at least should), the relationship and partnership between writers and editors shapes and forms what ultimately reaches the reader.

Because of this, all parties involved need to see the partnership of the writers and editors as a relationship, and the first key is communication. All relationships take time to develop, and editors are often overworked, underpaid, and under-appreciated.

If you are a writer, I strongly suggest spending some time and developing your skills as an editor. It will both help your writing, and help you appreciate the partnership. It's also a good way to hone your skills and generate revenue if you do it well.

If you are looking to develop professionally as an editor, you will likely spend time both working for other businesses and freelancing. You likely are a writer as well. Most editors specialize in one or two areas of editing. If you are a writer looking to understand this piece of the business, consider all of these different types of editing:

- Evaluation and Critique Editing: This is more of a general review and feedback about the overall health of the manuscript, from the material, the style, the grammatical quality, flow, structure, and the overall quality of the work. This can come from paid services, critique groups and writing partners.

- Developmental/Project Editing: The process of working with third parties to take an idea and develop a plan for the entire project, review of content and story development, and overall craft as an author.

- Substantial/Structural Editing: This can be seen as an overhaul and rework of your source material to fix problems in style, structure, and copy as needed.

- Stylistic/Line Editing: This is the process of taking your work and cleaning off the rough edges by a thorough review of terms, language, and tone, and smoothing out your message.

- Copy Editing: This is common mechanical editing and standardization of grammar, spelling, punctuation, formatting and style.

- Proofreading: This happens after all other editing processes, and is a final review of content, formatting, artwork, and overall review of the content and appearance of the book in preparation for release.

- Mock-Up/Roughing: More of a prototyping process than true editing, it is a process of roughing the layout and images with text to structure the appearance and flow of the copy with images. This is common in graphic intensive development, such as training materials, magazines and websites.

- Mark-Up/Coding: This process is geared to structure formatting, typically for use with specific writing and publishing tools.

- Formatting: This process ensures consistency throughout the work and structuring the appearance and flow, including fonts, sizes, headings, margins, and inclusion of graphics.

- Production Editing: Integration of copy, graphics, formatting, indexing, and going through mock-up and prototyping with all involved contributors to the final product. (This is common in graphic intensive development, such as training materials, magazines, comics, and websites.)

- Rewrite Editing: The process of taking parts of source material, including research and developed content to produce a new original work.
- Indexing: The process of taking key concepts and building the table of contents, index, and dictionary.
- Reference/Fact Checking: A separate review and editing process of verifying citations and material sourcing in an original work for factuality, correctness, and determination of citation and fair use. This may also involve a legal review of the material.
- Researching: Though not strict editing, the editor may do additional research to either validate the material and references or perform research to better detail individual components of the original work.
- Photo/Image/Artwork Research: Review and determination of images and artwork for inclusion in the original work, placement, and ensuring the work used is legally available for the use.

Many of these tasks are not pure editing, it's true, but depending on the types of original work and materials you edit, you will be called on to perform many of these functions. You can also see there is a degree of crossover between types of editing. The end result is ensuring the author releases the highest quality work they are prepared to do.

Beta Readers/Critique Partners

Of all the greatest challenges any creator faces is the harsh truth: You cannot see work through anyone else's eyes but your own. Beta readers and critique partners give you a different viewpoint, and a sample insight into your readers. You should not use people with whom you exchange bodily fluids or share DNA as your primary critique partners. You need people who will be fair and honest in their assessments for good and bad.

You need people who understand your genre that are fair and willing to give honest opinions and feedback and are not worried about having to sit across from you at the holiday dinner. Or can kill you in your sleep.

Editorial reminder: Beta readers cannot and do not replace your editors. They are looking to give you big picture feedback, not checking to see if you followed style guides with your commas.

Agents

What does an agent do, and do you need one?

The relationship between the author/artist and the agent is a business partnership but is also often described as being much like a marriage. And like any partnership, the two parties must operate in congruence to be effective. A bad one can be disastrous. Finding an agent can also be much like getting into a relationship; it takes a lot of dating before two people can form the right sort of bond.

All of this means taking your time and doing what needs to be done.

Where to start?

Do your homework:

- Research the industry to find out who represents your type of work. It does not do any good to submit your historical fiction to an agent who represents romance novels or how-to books.

- Research the market to determine the commercial viability of your work. Like every other facet of the business world, people's tastes change, and hot markets get quickly saturated.

- Research agents you are interested in. What is their industry experience? Are they responsive and professional in their communication? Are they excited about you and your work? What do others have to say about them in the industry publications and websites? Are they accepting submissions?

- Once you have a list of agents you are interested in pursuing:
  o Read and understand their submission guidelines. Follow them. Period.
  o Make sure they are accepting submissions.
  o Professionally package your submission. This means having:
  o A solid query letter. Keep it short and to the point.
  o A synopsis. Clearly and concisely describe the work. This will differ depending on the genre and industry.
  o A proposal. Nonfiction work is often sold based on a proposal, and not a finished work. For example, if you have a specific expertise in network security and wish to develop a book for professional development, it would include the outline, target audience, and sample chapters. The fiction proposal may be for a book series, and include the characters and storyline.
  o Sample chapters. When trying to sell your writing and yourself, the agent will want to see your style and skill level.
  o Finished work. If requested, the agent will want the finished work to review.

- o Be patient. We have become accustomed to immediate response and gratification. In the publishing industry, like many others, people are inundated with requests on a daily basis, and despite popular belief, they are not just waiting for you. It is not uncommon for it to take months for someone to get to your submission for review, and it will be one of many. Make sure your submission does not give them a reason to reject you out of hand, just to trim the list. This is common for agents, publishers, editors, and pretty much everyone in the business.
- You have an agent interested in signing you. What should you look for?
  - o What is their industry experience?
  - o Are they a member of the Association of Authors' Representatives (AAR)?
  - o Are they responsive and professional in their communication?
  - o Are they excited about you and your work?
  - o What do others have to say about them in the industry publications and websites?
  - o How experienced are they in dealing with book contracts and intellectual property?
  - o Are they charging something other than the standard fifteen percent?
  - o Is there anything you are not sure about or comfortable with?

You finally manage to find an agent. What are they really going to do for you? As an industry standard, they are getting fifteen percent of your check, and every check related to that work from now until the end of time.

You should be asking yourself what they are doing to earn it. Your agent may be very enthusiastic about you and your work, but if they cannot sell it, not only are you not earning anything, they aren't either. Your agent should:

- Be a cheerleader for you and your product.
- Know the business and the industry and protect you both from your publishers as well as yourself. They should make sure your best interests are represented.
- Be committed to your work and trying to sell it. Know how much of their time and resources they are investing to sell your work, and not someone else's. Keep in mind, this is not an exclusive relationship, and effective agents represent many quality people.

- Open doors to which you as an individual author would not have access. Experienced agents have relationships with publishers, editors, and the people that buy work. Many publishing houses only accept submissions from agents. They do this as a filter, and based on the relationship someone has with an agent, it gives the publisher some idea on the type and quality of work they are bringing through the door. It is in the best interest of the agent to only bring quality work to publishers, and only work that may be seriously considered by that house.
- Know the trends in the genres they represent and guide the author on trends and genres that are selling and what submissions publishing houses are actively soliciting.
- Advise you on your work, and give feedback on your style, quality, and developing your best commercial product.
- They are a partner and, in many ways, a business manager and a mentor helping you navigate the industry. They should be active in your dealings with publishers, and if necessary, the bad guy on your behalf. As a creator of material, your relationship with the publisher, editors, and artists for your product needs to remain open and professional. When problems arise, your agent should be the one to resolve it.
- Improve your query letters, proposals, pitches, and ultimately help you prepare to sell yourself and your work. Your agent can open doors, but at the end, you have to be ready to close the deal. If your agent can't sell a piece of work, they should be able to explain why, and help you understand the conditions. Sometimes it is simply the market. Other times, it could be the style or material. Either way, your agent should be open and direct about any and all rejections.
- Be experienced with publishing contracts. As complicated as many contracts can be, publishing and intellectual property rights are a specialty and can have unique (i.e. downright bizarre) clauses and language. They also are your representative, and work to give you the best possible contract possible. It is in their best interests as well.

It is worth noting what agents do not do.
- They are not your editor, though they can provide feedback and guidance.
- They are not your attorney, though they should be able to give experienced counsel.
- They cannot guarantee anything will sell or for how much.
- They cannot guarantee your success.

In short, your agent should represent you and your work, and be prepared to guide and protect you in the wild west of publishing. In an ideal world, it is the collaboration of the creator of content, and the one who manifests interest in that creation.

Back to our original question. Do you need an agent?

You are the only one who can answer that for yourself. It depends on your goals in the publishing industry, the services, and the type of work you want to do. If you intend to have even a moderately serious career as a writer in certain areas and genres, an agent is your partner in the writing business, and can open doors you will not be able to yourself.

If you do decide to pursue getting an agent, do your research, and make sure you understand the nature of the relationship.

Visual Artists

Most people are highly visual, and as a result, the art and graphics that accompany work are often the initial hook for potential readers. In many mediums, artwork is as critical as the writing, and at the minimum the artwork will give visual life to your words.

Consider all of these different needs for artwork:

- Cover Art: Whether a book is electronic or physical, the cover design is the first thing most people see, and can determine the level of success of a given title. Often, publishers will change the cover artwork or have multiple covers for a book to maximize attention. If you have a title that is not selling, consider a change in artwork and design.

- Logos/Brands: As discussed in the section on "Being your Brand," having a logo, pictures of yourself, and other images is critical so people can immediately connect to you and your work at a glance.

- Supporting images: Whether an article, a blog post, a technical manual, or even fiction, artwork backs up and emphasizes the material of the text. It could be pictures in a travel guide, icons to mark key points, reference maps, or other images that reinforce the work.

- Blog/Website Art: As a part of branding, you will want distinctive images that attract interest and inform people about what they can find on the site without being distracting or misleading.

- Marketing Materials: As with any business, people cannot buy a product they are not aware of. This is detailed elsewhere, but your artwork should connect all of the above with business cards, banners and advertisements to create unified campaigns to build your brand.

- Video: Many books now feature video either in partnership with the written work or as an advertising medium.

It is likely you will have other needs for artists and artwork in other ways as well.

Voice Artists/Producers

In the publishing world, audio books and narration of materials are a growing industry. Technology to record and edit your own work is affordable, and there are a lot of options in self-publishing or for work, both as an author and a narrator.

The ability to produce and edit audio and video are valuable technical skills related to audiobooks, social media advertising, podcasting, and video.

Publishers

At the end of the chain bringing your work brought to life and getting the finished work to the consumer. The traditional way of doing this is by going through a publisher.

So, what is a publisher, and what do they actually do?

First and foremost, publishers are a business whose goal is to make a profit. As an author, it will serve you well to know and understand what the publisher does, and why. Also know, if you go the self-publishing route you are taking on all of these jobs and roles as a part of the publishing process.

Even small and medium sized publishing houses will receive hundreds, if not thousands of manuscripts every year to ultimately publish maybe one or two percent of the submissions. This is one of the ways an agent can get you more consideration. Accepting and deciding to purchase a work means the publisher is creating an obligation and committing to significant expenses up front to turn your work into a finished product.

Once the publisher has opted to acquire the rights to your work, the process is just beginning. The terms of the agreement have to be accepted by all parties, and written into the contract. Remember, though the publisher is the one writing and presenting the contract, it is up to the author with the assistance of their agent and legal counsel to accept the terms or not, and to negotiate.

Before the ink has dried on the contract, the publisher begins planning and scheduling publication. Like all businesses, resources are limited, and the publisher has to maximize their use of them for not only your work, but for all the authors and works in their stable.

As discussed in the Editing section, there are many forms of editing, and working with your publisher, you and your editors will polish and create your final written product.

Between you and many people within the publisher, they will finalize the artwork. Art directors will support covers and interior design. (You may not even see the cover until the book is published.)

Layout and design will vary depending on your medium and topic/genre. Newspapers, magazines and other periodicals run on tight schedules and budgets, and typically within specific guidelines. Books and manuals can have a greater level of variance, but within each series there are typical standards. Think about the "For Dummies" series of books.

Fact checking and legal review are a big component of many non-fiction works and in media. Even if something is factual, your publisher may elect not to allow some content to be published under their name due to concerns about liability or simple controversy.

More editing. Just when you think your product is ready to go out the door, there is something else to change.

As your work moves into international markets, publishers in different regions may purchase the rights and take responsibility for translation and editing into other languages.

When all parties are satisfied, you move into the production phase. This includes generation of printed material, digital copies, audio, and multimedia. In fact, multiple publishers may be involved where one owns the print rights and another the audio.

Even before the work is available for sale, marketing and promotion efforts begin. The publisher will have varying levels of support for this and may go from press releases and providing signage and bookmarks to advertising campaigns.

Depending on the rights your publisher has, they will be responsible for distribution through multiple channels. This means getting work to online and retail locations in physical and digital forms. This also determines what regions your publisher can make your material available. You may have one publisher for the United States, a second for Canada, and another for European markets.

In addition to making your work available through their distribution channels, publishers may have their own sales staff actively marketing their catalog of works to wholesalers and retailers.

And finally, publishers will both do direct marketing and promotion of your work and provide authors with materials for promotional purposes. ((Expect to be responsible for the majority of your promotion!)

As you evaluate your relationship and contract with your publisher, you need to consider and understand all of the functions and level of commitment from the publisher for these duties, and your responsibilities as well. All of these should be specified in the contract.

If you elect to purse self-publishing, you are accepting not only all of these functions, but also the financial risks as well and should plan accordingly.

Publicists

I'll say this several times. Obscurity is the enemy of the author.

A Publicist is a person or company that specializes in one thing: creating awareness. You may also hear this referred to as public relations.

Much like agents, publicists have specialties both in terms of types of media and genres they work with. Often, they have specialties in the types of media services they provide.

I was in a chat with several fellow authors the other day, and the question came up if anyone had used a publicist and what they could actually do for you. It wound up being a fun conversation. Being a business and technical guy at heart, and more of an extrovert than not, I wanted to help push some of my fellow writers forward.

Depending on your personality and goals, if you hire a publicist, you need to be open and honest about what you want, need, and what you are willing to do, or not to further your business and career goals. I asked a couple of questions, and one of my more introverted friends was nervous at the thought of even speaking to the publicist, much less what they as they author might need to be asked to do.

As with editors, even if your publisher provides services from a publicist, you may want to investigate hiring one of your own. Much like agents, publicists tend to have specific industry expertise, specialties, relationships and genres they support.

Publicists may be engaged to support a specific launch, or in the longer term to support a series and grow your brand.

What can you expect from a publicist? Different ones provide different levels of service, and you should evaluate this relationship in much the same way you would in researching agents and editors. The approach a particular publicist uses, and the relationships they have coupled with enthusiasm for you and your work will have a big influence on the success of their efforts.

What services should the publicist be able to provide you?

- Work with you to develop your platform and your brand strategy. Their experience can help you understand the market, and what typically is effective in your market and in congruence with your goals.
- Guide the strategy, design and content of your website, blog, and social media presence.
- Develop and disseminate press releases.
- Sculpt your biography and public persona.
- Facilitate and solicit reviews, endorsements and blurbs for your work, and for the marketing materials.
- Review, advise and oversee book covers, blurbs, and synopses with reference to your marketing efforts.
- Have the industry knowledge and relationships to pitch interviews, feature articles, blog tours, book tours, and appearances for your target audience.
- Plan your launch strategy, launch events, talking points and materials.
- Advise on events and venues to target for marketing your work.
- Suggest and promote your work for profiles, lists, award nominations, and other public recognition.
- Create media kits on your website and social media as well as the packages for specific product launches.
- Evaluate and coach you on your public persona, your brand, and how to grow and mature your public self.
- Provide feedback about how you and your work are being received and help adjust the message as necessary.

When you are evaluating publicists, you are looking for someone who knows and understands your market and its rules, understands its nuances, and has the relationships to maximize awareness of you, your brand, your message and your product.

Webmaster

Many people now have the capabilities to build their own website, or at least a blog. As one of the primary tools of connecting with your fans and customers, it is the flagship of your brand and real estate you own and control. Make sure it represents you.

Having a good blog and a good website extends beyond technical capabilities. A good webmaster not only saves you the time of maintaining your site, like a cover artist they have aesthetic skills in terms of design and flow and the ability to design to meet your business needs. They will have tools and knowledge that can save you time and money in the design and construction process.

This is one area where you should lean on the expertise of others and support their business while they support yours.

Social Media Manager

Now you're just going off the rails. A social media manager? Isn't social media how I connect with people?

When you get to the portion of this book on social media, and other references, you will learn a few things. There is much more to social media than shouting "Buy my book!" from the rooftops. Social media also famously can be a tremendous time waste.

The key to social media is balance. Yes, it can be a fantastic way to connect with friends, fans and potential customers and grow those relationships. It's also a good way to spend hours of quality writing time looking at cat videos and writing memes.

Services include scheduling social media posts, keeping up with your social media presence, and responding to general inquiries. You can respond to more personal exchanges, and post information such as pictures with fans at events, or news stories relevant to your work. The goal is to spend your time where only you can.

Financial and Business Services

At the end of it all are the service providers for business and financial services. This will range from your accountants and CPA's handling your taxes to products and services in advertising, printing, and all the other professional services every business needs.

Achieving Goals

"I believe the process of going from confusion to understanding is a precious, even emotional, experience that can be the foundation of self-confidence."
-Brian Greene

All of us have set up goals for the new year at some point in our lives. Work out more, lose weight, stop smoking. All too often, we watch them float away on the wind, gone until the next new year.

Why do we fail? Because we don't change our mindset to believe it can be done, and therefore we fail to act.

This is not a unique idea. It's a fundamental truth.

You can find many techniques for developing goals and executing them. Fundamentally, it distills down to these elements:

- Set your goal.
- Write it down.
- Break it into a list of specific tasks and deliverables.
- Develop a plan.
- Focus on the tasks that need to be done when they need to be done.
- Execute.
- Learn from your mistakes and do it again.

I realize this sounds simplistic, and it is. At the same time, it really can be this simple.

The first step is creating and setting realistic and achievable goals.

I was part of a panel on developing a book project a while back. After the panel, one of the audience members was interested in developing her life story into a book and had no idea where to start. This person had no experience writing and really didn't know where to start.

I've had similar questions over the years regarding books, technology projects, and even startup companies. Here are the core recommendations I gave the person.

They were interested in sharing their personal story as a message of hope for others but were concerned about how to go about it. They had done little writing outside of school. The idea of writing a book seemed a large task.

We sat down for a few minutes, and outlined a path.

The first goal was to create a blog. The second was to write a blog post every Friday with whatever they felt they needed to share that week.

The purpose was to make a few small, easily achievable goals. They give an immediate return and take little investment beyond a little time. Through this exercise, they developed skills as a writer, and got the story out to the world.

For them, at the time, it was enough. If in time they decide to go the next step, it's much easier to go from articles and blog posts to a book than to have no skills, no plan, and a dream. It will also help them decide if writing is a medium of expression for them in the long term.

It's much like a person wanting to lose a hundred pounds. The number sounds daunting, and it's a lot harder to take the weight off than put it on. It takes time, work, and discipline. Building a book project or a business is the same way.

It is always one step at a time. Learn from your setbacks and mistakes, but do not let them stop you. Slow and steady is still progress. Not everyone is made to be a sprinter.

You cannot achieve anything until you take that first step. Write that first word. Have that first conversation.

Defining Success

Don't take 'no' when your gut tells you 'yes.'
- James Patterson

The idea of defining success is often buried in the details, and not called out when we talk about goals and objectives; goals are what you want to accomplish, success defines how well you met them. I've found it critical to be specific about what success means for any given piece of work, both for myself and any partners or clients. As this is your plan, your business, and your exercise, I challenge you to define success for yourself. This is where you can detail your personal ideas and goals, as well as what you call out more publicly.

You must be the one to decide what you are satisfied with in your work. Define your success. It is much harder to achieve what you cannot envision.

Your goals include defining what you are doing and delivering for your customers. Now it's time for you to define success for yourself.

Here's some questions you should be able to answer:

- What if I don't deliver on everything I promised my customers/ readers/patrons?
- Is my expectation to make a living from the work, or just supplemental income?
- What if I don't make as much money as I expect on the project?
- Can I afford to lose what I'm investing?
- Aside from the financial gain, what other benefits am I expecting? Fame? Notoriety? More speaking engagements? More publishing opportunities? More places to sell my work? New business and personal relationships?

Once you answer the basic business questions, we have to look at what is often more important than financial or business indicators. You are a creator. You bring new ideas to life and give your own spin to old ones. More important are these factors in defining success:

- Is it worth publishing the work if only one person finds value in it?
- Is success just holding your work in your hand, or seeing it on the shelf of a store?
- Are you looking for a literary award or other recognition from your peers?

Businesses and projects fail every day.

This is different.

If nothing else, ask yourself this question: was there enough value having taken the journey and completed the work worth it? Is it enough to create a body of work you are proud of and love? Your work can last long after you are gone. Many famous authors and artists never found acclaim in their lifetimes, achieving fame and notoriety only after death.

This book is aimed at people pouring themselves in a very personal way into their work. By no means am I taking away anything from the person who opens a flower shop, bookstore, gallery or garbage collection company. The people who invest themselves in any business do so with everything in their being.

What I am saying is that unlike other businesses, being a writer, artist, or even a game developer can carry a next level of personal investment. Your art carries a piece of you into the world in a very personal way, more than any other business opportunity. The florist creates art through arrangement, it's true, but it's temporary and fluid. Even garbage collection has a certain creativity to it, in determining business process and how you brand your business.

This section of the plan really is for you and your team. For you, by you. And it helps to make sure your core team, even if it's just you, are aware of what you really want to come from your work.

You can explore the good and the bad, your dreams and nightmares. Call them out, so you can manage them and deal with them.

Resistance

"Any change, even a change for the better, is always accompanied by drawbacks and discomforts."
- Arnold Bennett

When dealing with electricity, there are two important, if inverse concepts; resistance and conductivity. Resistance is a measure of the difficulty for electrical current to flow through a material. Conductivity is a measure of how easily the material can carry current.

You may ask what this has to do with business or writing?

We all face resistance every day. Whether our lives are resistant or conductive is largely a result of our mindsets, and how we approach our work and lives.

Resistance comes in many forms: writer's block, listening to negative feedback and letting it become a distraction, allowing the challenges of life to beat us down, or taking the easy path and not following our dreams. Sometimes it seems the universe itself is out to get us, such as a car wreck or illness taking away from our creative time. Other times, we bring it onto ourselves by looking for the negativity in everything or expecting to fail.

Have you ever noticed when things start going well, too well, that something will happen and get in your way? Have you ever heard of a self-fulfilling prophecy? If you believe bad things will happen, are your expectations met if not exceeded?

All of this is resistance.

Yes, there's a lot of books and programs out there around the principles of positive thought. I believe it to be we find ways to self-sabotage and take advantage of the times when things go wrong to make sure we dig ourselves a deeper hole.

But I also know success propagates success.

Our mindset, whether positive or negative, determines how we will deal with the challenges we are presented both in our lives, and our businesses. Success or failure is determined by how we react to those events.

Your story may be rejected by a publication. Do you look at it as failure, or that it wasn't a good fit? Do you take feedback as criticism or critique to learn from?

I invite you to find ways to embrace a conductive life. When you have a success, celebrate it. When something doesn't go to plan, don't take it as a failure. Learn from what you didn't anticipate and look for the opportunity it may provide.

An accident could put you in contact with a true fan when you're sitting in the shop waiting on a repair. A long line at lunch can turn into a book sale, or the inspiration for a story. A rejection can still put you on the radar for a publisher or an agent.

You will face resistance. It won't always be easy. But know this, you only face your challenges alone if you choose to.

So how do we do this?

In electricity, resistance and conductivity are determined by two things: material (what it's made of) and geometry (the shape and size). A given wire can only carry so much energy and output. If you need more power to flow through a line, you have to go to a more conductive material, or increase the diameter of the wire.

In life and business, it's the same. When faced with a challenge, how you react will define you, your image, and your brand. If you can't increase your capacity and output, you need to find the people and tools to help, or risk overload and burnout.

But once you overcome the resistance, you can shine brighter than ever.

aMuse Me – Paying Dues to the Muse

"This is the other secret that real artists know and wannabe writers don't. When we sit down each day and do our work, power concentrates around us. The Muse takes note of our dedication. She approves. We have earned favor in her sight. When we sit down and work, we become like a magnetized rod that attracts iron filings. Ideas come. Insights accrete."

- *Steven Pressfield, The War of Art: Break Through the Blocks & Win Your Inner Creative Battles*

"Don't pressure me," said the writer to the muse. "I'm not feeling it today."

Muse raised her eyebrow. "Prima Donna," snipped the creative spirit, and flitted away.

That would be a true story. Or almost.

The myth of the Muses comes from the Greeks. According to the poet Hesiod, Zeus and Mnemosyne had nine daughters, and each was the inspiration for a different art or science:

- Calliope (epic poetry - writing tablet)
- Clio (history - scroll)
- Euterpe (lyric poetry - aulos, a Greek flute)
- Thalia (comedy and pastoral poetry - comic mask)
- Melpomene (tragedy - tragic mask)
- Terpsichore (dance - lyre)
- Erato (love poetry - cithara, a Greek type of lyre)
- Polyhymnia (sacred poetry - veil)
- Urania (astronomy - globe and compass)

Six centuries later, the Roman scholar Varro pared them down to three:
- Melete (practice)
- Mneme (memory)
- Aoide (song)

Regardless of the time or tradition, humanity has often credited creativity and innovation to an external force. Who am I to argue?

What I believe is important is naming it gives us a key to the psychology behind inspiration and allows us to embody our pursuits. (And provides someone to blame the days we stare blankly at the paper, the screen, or the clay tablet.)

We may today be less inclined to blame Calliope for not showing up in the morning, than calling it writer's block. No matter what we call it, we have all felt it at times.

So, what do we do about it?

I once heard Chelsea Quinn Yarborough comment on how she beats writer's block. She said, "I look at the stack of unpaid bills and get to work."

Among things you can do to make the most productive use of your creative time:

- Have a routine and a schedule when you work. Yes, I called it work instead of writing, editing, etc. Treat it like your business, and train yourself to know when it's time to produce.
- Train the body, and the mind will follow. If you need a cup of coffee, music in the background, or to spend fifteen minutes working out to get your mind and body pumping, make it part of your routine. If you have a variable schedule, and cannot always have a set time, this can be even more important by putting you into the right frame of mind faster.
- Have targets any time you sit down to work, be it time or word count. It feeds the reward centers of the brain and helps with the mindset. When you reach your target, have some sort of reward to incentivize you to stay on track.
- If you do sit down to a blank page, have writing prompts handy. The act of putting words on paper, even if it's just copying a few paragraphs from a favorite story or a relevant piece of research material can jump start you.
- Find the writing strategy that works for you, but I strongly suggest having an outline, notes, or even a formal structure to work from. It helps get you on track, keeps you there and takes away the blank page.
- Turn off easy distractions, Facebook, etc. Separate your writing time from your research time, so that if you wind up in a rabbit hole chasing the latest news, it has less effect on your production time.
- When it is time to work, come prepared to work. Set aside the drama of life.
- When you get an idea or inspiration, write it down. Keep it somewhere. You never know when you'll need it.

If you get into a routine, treat it like your business, your profession, the muses will be much more likely to want to come to you.

Yes, many of these are easier said than done, but if you wait to write when inspiration strikes, you will find yourself writing in short, frantic bursts with long periods in the doldrums. If you plan to write as the focus of your business, or even as a cornerstone with your blogs and articles, you cannot afford to wait for the muse to strike. You have content to produce.

There will be the days the words flow to the page like water from the wheel. Other days, it can be a battle of the blank page. Not every word will be gold, but remember, it is easier to edit than to stare at the white screen.

Imposter Syndrome

"I have written 11 books but each time I think 'Uh-oh, they're going to find out now. I've run a game on everybody, and they're going to find me out.'"
—Maya Angelou

The lights in the packed auditorium dimmed slightly. The last few whispers died down as Helen Lang, the speaker, strode from behind the screen and approached the podium.

Jack put on a smile for his students and leaned back in the stadium seat. *If only I could do that,* he mused as he studied the speaker's long smooth stride and confident poise. *It kills me every time I have to speak to my class. I wish…I wish I was articulate. Confident. Smart. If only…it would launch my career to the next level. I could do more than struggle through one class at a time. But who would listen to me? Why?*

Just a few minutes earlier…

Helen peeked around the corner of the curtain at the packed room. People were even having to stand from the lack of chairs. *Why are there so many here just to listen to me?*

She pried her hands away from the draped fabric, leaving behind most of the dampness from her palms. What if they figure out I'm a fraud? My work is just derivative of Doctor Amar's work. He's the one that should be up here. Not me. She took a deep breath, raised her head and stepped into the spotlight.

Does this sound familiar? Either or both situations?

Jack was losing the battle to peel the smile from his face. He was barely listening, amazed at how much she had accomplished in her few years of work. Even his students kept glancing in his direction. *They are realizing how star struck I am. I'll never get them to pay attention to me again. Why did I offer extra credit for them to come hear the talk?*

Almost there, she thought. If only I hadn't stumbled over half the presentation. Helen imagined half the audience had left by now, embarrassed for her research.

Do you wonder how others perceive you?

Jack clapped his hands at the close of the presentation. He'd been the first to start, but by a millisecond. *Even if I've lost the class for myself*, he mused, *they've gotten a semester's education in the last hour.*

Helen forced the smile on her face and gave a small bow, resisting the urge to bolt from the stage. *I wasn't even done when they started clapping. I was pretty much closed out, but I didn't get to all of my acknowledgements. If only I didn't have to go to the reception... maybe it was so bad, no one will show up, except for the free drinks.*

Have you doubted your every move?

Jack's students grinned as they followed him into the reception hall. Let them laugh. His heart fluttered as he tried to get up the courage to speak to her, but he must. He has to at least congratulate her. Maybe even a little of her success will rub off on him. Several students are asking to follow along. *I'd hoped to do this in private so they wouldn't see how excited I am. They must be wanting to continue to watch the show.*

A dozen people crowded around her, polite smiles on their faces. *Hadn't they sat through the same presentation she'd struggled through, again?* Her heart pounded as a large crowd approached... oh no...

Jack stopped, reached out his hand, hoping it wasn't too clammy. "That is impressive work, Doctor Lang. I don't know if you remember --"

Helen's heart thudded. "Doctor Amar, so good to see you. I wish I'd known you were here. I'd never have done it without all your amazing work." She looked into the fresh faces of his students, one of whom she'd been not that many years ago. *She'd been lucky to get into his class... he was so tough and only taught one session a semester.*

Do you even question your own successes and accomplishments?
It's called Imposter Syndrome.
We compare. All. The. Time.
We compare ourselves to our peers. Our families. To our bosses. To celebrities. To experts. To our neighbors and friends.
And we think we come up short.
There is a quote I try to keep in mind all of the time.
Confidence isn't walking into a room thinking you are better than everyone else, it's walking in and not needing to compare yourself to anyone.
Are you ready to be confident? Self-assured? Ready to take on and succeed in the challenges of life?
 You have to change your way thinking. Embrace a different mindset.
1. Stop feeding your need to be liked. Face the facts that not everyone is going to come and worship you, and that's ok. Embracing who you truly are will attract those who are meant to be in your life, and you in theirs.

2. Stop comparing yourself to others. That nagging voice in your head? It's not you. It's everyone around you. It's your parents, grandparents, friends, detractors, colleagues, media, etc. who are looking to hold themselves back through their fears and push them on you too.

I repeat, it's not you.

Decide what YOU want. Live not out of obligation, or someone else's expectations. Living the life you truly desire is not a sin. Putting your wants, needs, desires and expectations onto someone else is selfish.

1. Accountability is key. Realize what you do well and OWN it. Acknowledge your shortcomings and OWN them.
2. Expand your mind. Learn, study, and be willing to question the world around you.
3. Be bold. Take the leap of faith. Say yes to opportunities, new adventures, take risks.

Our attitudes and the paths of our lives are determined by the people we surround ourselves with and the experiences we have. The more time and action you take in driving the direction you want to go, the more confident you will become, and the more fulfilling life you will have.

You are not an impostor. You have unique views, knowledge and experience. Add to it. Grow.

Overnight Success

People assume they are most creative at a certain age. But if you look at truly great artists, they always get better.
- Jeff Koons

We hear many stories about overnight successes. We hear about the actor or actress discovered walking down the street or working in a coffee shop. Musicians discovered at an open mic night. Writers whose first book was a New York Times bestseller.

We have all heard the story of J. K. Rowling being broke, heading towards poverty when an eight-year-old girl read the first chapter of Harry Potter and demanded the next. Without Alice Newton, daughter of publishing house Bloomsbury's chairman, Rowling would likely have had her thirteenth rejection.

What do they all have in common? You may answer, "Luck."

In a way that is true. Random chance does play a role.

In my experience, a true "overnight success" who stepped from unknown into the bright lights by chance is less common than unicorns. You have a greater likelihood of winning the Powerball than having someone randomly pick up your manuscript in a coffee shop and turn you into a best seller.

Here are the most important lessons I have learned from successful people, whether the overnight variety or not:

- Luck is created, not found.
- Be willing to take risks and say "Yes."
- Success comes from practicing, honing your talents and skills and using them to create work.
- Placing yourself where and when you have opportunities to introduce and expose yourself and your work to potential fans and customers. Change your routines. If you go to the same places at the same times, you will usually see the same people with the same results.
- Give your efforts time to develop and mature. Study your successes and failures. When all else fails, make conscious changes.
- Keep a positive attitude. Your mood and attitude influence those you attract, and those you push away.
- We all have times when we question and doubt ourselves and our work. This is normal and healthy and makes sure we look at it critically to produce our best work. It's when we get into a spiral of negativity and hyper-criticality that we wind up wasting time, and potentially give up.
- Accept honest critiques and learn from them.

On top of everything else—never quit, never give up. Each rejection give you feedback and puts you one step closer to success.

There's the old story about the prospector who went west to pursue his fortunes. A geologist, he studied the landscape, and found the claim he wanted to buy. Spending most of his resources in the process, he used the claim as collateral to buy the mining equipment he needed.

For months on end, he dug into the hill. Seeing every sign that gold really was in the hill, and even finding a few flakes, he kept digging day after day. Finally hitting the day, he could go no further, he sold his equipment and the mine to his financial backer.

Convinced at the value of the mine, he hired the prospector to assist, and they continued to dig. One day and a foot-deep pilot hole in the side of the mine, they struck a rich vein. The backer increased his wealth and the prospector walked away with a day's wage.

If you take time to study successful people, especially the overnight successes, you will find they did the work, and opened themselves to possibilities. Even when they hit inevitable challenges, they picked up their tools and went to work the next day. You never know the day you'll strike gold.

Are you ready for the real surprise?

Overnight success can be more of a curse than a blessing. It can even be a disaster.

I can hear the voices in the wild. "That's a curse I'd take." or "It's a problem I'd love to have."

How can success be a burden? Consider professional athletes. Look at how many rocket to stardom surrounded by people. Too soon, the ride is over through injury or other factors, and they are broke and alone.

It can be much harder to be successful than a failure.

As your success grows, so do the pressures:

- Every new piece of work will be compared to everything you have already done.
- More people will want your time and attention.
- More people are watching you, not only professionally but personally.
- You may find you have to question everyone you meet, and their motives.
- More income and notoriety mean more responsibilities, more travel, more appearances.

None of what I say here should scare or dissuade you, but remind you of the possibility. While you go through the process of building your career, establishing relationships, and making connections are some of the tools that will help you mature and be successful. Being a writer is not an individual enterprise. It's a team sport.

The Emotional Investment in Your Work

"Have no fear of perfection -- you'll never reach it."
- Salvador Dali

Of everything else in this book, the hardest challenge most creative people face is when our work meets the adoring (or not so much) public.

No matter what you create, whether it's a song, a book, a painting, anything you are taking from your mind to bring to market, eventually others will see it. Much like a newborn child, as the parent of the product: you have poured your heart and soul into your work. You have great pride in its completion.

Now comes the hard part.

You need to set that part of yourself that is emotionally tied to the work aside, lock it in a closet, and don't let it out until you have taken a critical and honest look at the end result. (Don't forget to feed creativity, we'd hate for it to starve to death.) I usually first do this when I move into editing mode.

I'm not suggesting you do this in the search for perfection, because you'll never get there. You can always improve on any work, even a masterpiece. You also don't do this to engage in self-abuse or question the value of what you've done.

You need to separate yourself from the emotional attachment long enough to use a critical eye and see if your work is ready for prime time. To ask yourself, is it ready to go to market?

More importantly, once your baby hits the marketplace, you need to be able to separate your attachment from the work, because no matter how good it is, someone isn't going to like or resonate with it. In some cases, all they may see is the cover, subject, or tagline, and decide they hate it.

Just say no to trolls.

We as creators want everyone to love and adore those things we bring to the world as much as we do. It's just never going to happen. You can't create something that is all things to all people. You just have to work to make sure your product finds the people who will make it part of their world.

2: The Foundation

Building the Foundation

"You read a book from beginning to end. You run a business the opposite way. You start with the end and then you do everything you must to reach it."
- *Harold S. Geneen*

Developing a story can be a lot like starting up a business. You get an idea, and then you start into your process. Plotters begin to outline, build a framework, and then flesh in the details. Pantsers can sit down and start writing, working their own way through the story. Most of us are somewhere in between.

Plotters are also more likely to finish a story, find and plug the holes as they go along, and have much less editing and cleanup to do.

When we tell a story, we have long been told the questions it should answer; "Who, What, When, Where, Why and How."

I'm not going to debate the merits of plotting vs. pantsing, because I've done both in my writing. But when it comes down to your business, there's only one option. You need to have a plan.

I just felt the collective groan.

I can almost hear you saying, "I just want to write!"

I want you to be writing too. Or editing, doing art, etc. I'm also assuming you bought this book to build the business side of your creative outlet, so you can do more of whatever it is you want to do. A proper foundation for your business will give you the tools for success, and should address these questions:

1. *Who* defines both the type of people you want to surround yourself with to support yourself and your business and the customers you wish to serve, but not necessarily the specific individuals. Over time, the people you work with may change, or even just what role they are filling, but there are always specific tasks that must be done. You also want to know who your audience isn't. It is just as important to know who your roadblocks are as it is to know your tribe and true fans.

2. *What* is often the key to success. What do you intend to do? What is the goal? What am I trying to accomplish? The end product? What are the risks? What are the rewards? What do I need to be successful? What benefit will you provide your customers? Your readers? Your vision for yourself in publishing is what gives you, and your business as an author, purpose.

3. *Where* is primarily a question we will address as a part of Operations but is still a consideration in building your foundation. Are you planning to travel? Do you intend to have a storefront or just exist in the virtual world? Where will the work be done? Where will we market and sell it?

4. *When* is also an operational question and tied to specific work over being the bedrock of your business. What is my timeline? The milestones? Is there a time box? An expiration date on the idea? A particular time it needs to be ready for an event? But, you must remember, over time, even the foundation of your business will need maintenance and repair. Sometimes it will even need to be rebuilt.

5. *Why* is the motivation behind your vision, gives you the strength and and the reason your readers and customers will come to you. Why am I and my team doing this? Why would someone find value and benefit from the results?

6. *How* defines the means and methods by which your business will work. Using all of the pieces and resources above, it's determining the approach to execute and deliver to meet your goals. How do you define success? How do you define failure?

The proper foundation must be strong enough to hold you and your business up in both good times and bad, but still give you the room to work on it when you need to. Think about it like a crawl space under your house. You don't really want to have to climb under there, but it is a lot easier to fix a leak than if the pipes are buried in concrete.

Once your foundation is complete, and you enter the business cycle, you should be ready to follow and execute on your plan. Then be ready to review, refine, and adapt it. Do more of what works and learn from what doesn't. And if this is for a particular project or activity, compare the end results with the plan. What did you get right? What didn't go as planned? What did you learn, and how do you change future work from the experience?

With your business, if you fly by the seat of your pants, you'll soon find the fly is open and the back door is drafty.

Your Business Plan

"I ain't Martin Luther King. I don't need a dream. I have a plan."
— Spike Lee

Business plans are outdated. Besides, I'm an author. Why do I need a business plan?

At least half of you had some version of this fly through your head when you saw the heading for the section.

It's true, as an author you're probably not out looking for venture capital or bank funding, and even if you are, large elaborate business plans the size of a college philosophy textbook are out of date. With consulting clients, I tell them, the plan isn't for them, it's for you.

Business plans are meant to force you to think about the stuff you want to avoid before it actually goes wrong. To quote Winston Churchill, *"Plans are of little importance, but planning is essential."*

If your writing style is to be a planner and a plotter, this will likely feel natural. If you're a pantser, I'll wait for you to pick up the book from where you just flung it into the wall.

I, for one, fall in between the styles for my books, and my version of plans.

Before we go any further, let's define a business plan. It's nothing more than putting down your vision (not dreams) for what you want to accomplish and a roadmap to get there. What benefits can it bring? A business plan helps:

- Remind you of what you want to do for myself, set realistic goals, and the benefit you bring your readers and customers.
- Determine what resources you need and make the most of your limited resources, including time and money.
- Organize what you need to do and when, and keep you on track.
- Correct your course when you've gotten off track.
- Forecast the benefits you expect from the fruits of your labors.
- See the challenges and obstacles in meeting your goals.
- Find the solutions to those challenges, especially when you're most stressed by them.
- Consider all sides, and decide if it's the right project, or the right time.
- Consider the risks and pitfalls, and plan for them if they happen.
- Make sure you don't miss or forget something in the process, that could cost you time, money, or both.

- Refine your project, so that you understand your market and your audience.
- Define and achieve success.
- Learn from your mistakes.

Much of my success in life is not due to having a plan, but because I plan for contingencies.

For many people, their idea of a career as an author is one where a person takes some time to throw content into a document, stick it on Amazon, and wait for the money to roll in. If you like, please give it a try. I'll be right here when you get back… and oh my, that was quick.

You may have heard numbers like 80% of small businesses fail in the first two years. For authors, sometimes it can feel like we have failed in the first few hours after a book lands on the market, after months or even years of work. It can even feel like we've failed before the first words hit the page.

It may seem obvious, but the reason most businesses fail, is because they run out of cash. This doesn't mean they weren't profitable.

Success and failure are but ways to describe a point in time. Both give you opportunities to learn and grow. And there is no absolute success or complete failure. It is a sliding scale that over time looks like roller coaster. You just have to take it for a ride. Long term success is learning to push through the times you land on your face, wipe off the dirt, and get back on the bike.

The golden rule of any project: anything that can go wrong, will go wrong, and at the worst possible time. Sometimes that means your laptop dies when you're fifteen words away from finishing the last edit when your deadline is in two hours. Sometimes family issues pull you away from your work when you were in the zone cranking out five thousand words an hour.

Life happens.

What's important is not what happens, it's how you react. If you let the challenges get to you, you can wind up losing hours or days to stress, and even more time catching up. Your plan can help you do all of this. It's your life preserver in a storm.

Let's talk about something that can be an even bigger crisis: *success*.

Did I just say success can be a problem? If you're not ready for it, yes.

What happens if your book all of a sudden becomes the newest hot property; the next Harry Potter, or 50 Shades?

Few of us are going to plan for it, and it's almost impossible to do at that level. But what happens if the Kickstarter you planned to raise $10,000 brings in $100,000 or more? It happens. Look into the story of the card game Exploding Kittens.

Instead of having to autograph and send out a hundred books, now you have to do thousands. If you promised some piece of SWAG, can you fulfill all of the requests?

Your plan makes you look at the most likely outcomes and how to get to where you want to go.

What Goes Into the plan?

There's a ton of templates out there. Most are overkill for what you need.

This book takes you through all of the pieces, you just need to fill in the blanks.

The most important parts of any plan are:

- The objective of the plan, be it a book, a series, or your career. This would vary depending on what you write, or the services you provide.
- The team of people involved in the project, including other authors, agents, artists, publishers, editors, and anyone key to your success.
- List of any contracts, key dates or deliverables.
- Market analysis to determine the current target market size and how to reach them.
- Your marketing and advertising strategy. This includes your reader avatar, defining your target market, keywords and lookalike audiences, and how you intend to reach them (in-person, paid advertising, etc.)
- Your operational plan, including all of the administrative work, such as applying for conventions, making sure ads are running and performing, and getting the writing done.
- Your financial plan, including a budget, expected revenues, how and where you intend to spend money to build your business and your brand.
- The list of all of the intellectual property you are developing (books, recordings, etc.) who holds rights to each, and the terms/reversion of rights parameters.

Yes, this does mean putting in some work, but it will save you both time and money in the long run.

You can find additional resources at **https://authoressentials.net**, including free templates!

Keep Trying

I said at the beginning of this book, if you don't try, you've already failed. I'm not saying to try everything, but to make a conscious decision about what makes sense for you. It's okay to lose. Sometimes things aren't going to work. Rejoice in your wins, learn from your losses.

Nothing is wasted unless you don't take the lesson from it.

I've done a lot of shows, events and conventions in my time, and will keep on doing it. Here's what I've learned.

- Be aware of your audience. Just because something worked last week, doesn't mean it will this week. The inverse is true. If you believe in something, keep trying and refining until it works, or you figure out why it doesn't.
- Know your market, and how it's changing.
- Have a thick skin. This can be tough, but being in front of an audience isn't always easy. Not everyone is going to share your tastes and desires, and that's okay. And some people are trolls that will never be happy.
- No trolls in the tribe! As you build both a fan base, and your network of people in the industry, you are going to meet people who may be jealous of your success, or simply hold you back because of their own failures. Other times, it may be due to differences of opinion that cause people who were once supportive of you to change sides and become a distraction or detractor. And you will come across people who simply enjoy causing trouble to watch the result. Give those people an option to either be supportive and grow with you, or boot them out post haste.
- Have a support group. You can't do it alone. Whether selling and doing business on-line or doing appearances, build relationships. Have fun and know who has your back. We all need a friend sometimes, and other times, you get to be that friend. Amazing things happen through connections.
- Cultivate and protect your persona.

And finally, a lesson I learned from all the years I lived flying from place to place. Take care of yourself first. You can't help others if you can't breathe.

Planning and Execution

"It does not do to leave a live dragon out of your calculations, if you live near him."
— J.R.R. Tolkien, *The Hobbit*

At the core of every plan is the problem you are trying to solve, or the product you are looking to deliver.

The first part of your plan will depend a little on whether this plan is designed to be your overall tool for all of your offerings, or if it's for a particular project. Keep in mind, if you are part of a writing partnership, but also have your own solo projects, you may want to manage each of those as separate plans depending on your needs.

If the plan is your overarching tool for your business, the summary would include:

- Project Name/Titles
- Principals - Who all are principal partners, such as Publishers, Co-authors , Contributors, Editors, and Artists.
- Responsible Agents - Anyone who is critical to your work, such as your Agent(s), Accountant, Manager, Public Relations, or Assistants.
- Objectives - What you intend to accomplish with this particular project.
- Summary - An overview of the project, methods of publication and distribution, and any other affiliated work.
- The project plan, including milestones and publication dates.

In your plan, this information serves to let anyone you are working with know the foundation of the project, who all of the key participants are, and the general approach for the project at a glance.

The Five P's

We have all heard the phrase, "Follow your passion." Our passions can also lead us to make quick decisions. Sometimes it works. Often, it doesn't.

Not only are you an artist, a creator, you also own a business. Passion is not enough to achieve long term success.

Too often, I've heard people preach about their passion for something. In fun motivational quotes to start your day: "find your purpose, live your passion, and you'll never work a day in your life."

Sounds great, right?

In my theory, there's the five P's. Passion, Planning, Purpose, Performance and Perseverance.

- Passion is the emotion that stokes the inner fire that illuminates your dreams and fuels your drive. It inspires your creativity and empowers you to chase your desires. Being so powerful, passion overpowers logic and reason. Sometimes to reach great heights, and sometimes sending us falling to great depths.

- Planning is the focus of much of this book. Once you know what you want to do, and why you are driven to do it, the plan gives you the tools to craft a map and a process to succeed.

- Purpose is the foundation on which we build our business and our lives. Our passions can lead us to identify and follow our life's purpose. It's the why and the what of our lives. Our purpose is the reason for our lives, and the benefit we can be to others.

- Performance is evaluating how you are doing against your plan, and against your peers and competitors. We measure our performance to understand how we are doing, and how we can improve.

- Perseverance is the mindset of success. An old quote is: "Eighty percent of life is showing up." Perseverance is what will keep us believing when the embers of passion have been doused, our purpose has been called into doubt, our plan hasn't worked, and we see others passing us.

So, what do those same people say to do? Live your life's purpose.

The most successful people are the ones who strike a balance of their life's purpose and their passions.

But how do they do it? What does it really mean?

Pretend you are on a camping trip, and you need to have a fire.

Through the need of your passion, you imagine the flames licking at the wood, the warm glow pushing back the darkness, and the heat chasing away the evening chill.

Planning for the long evening, you gather plenty of wood and kindling, and make sure the fire ring is safely away from your tent and any trees.

Now with purpose and vision, you build a fire ring, make a kindling bundle, and bring it to life with the strike of a match.

Evaluating the performance, is it at a roaring blaze in minutes, or are you tending to the few embers you have been able to bring to life?

What makes the difference in success?

Is it luck? Sometimes. But consistent long-term success means doing the work to build the fire, keep it stoked, and soak up its warmth. With a little perseverance, you can raise a roaring fire even in a storm.

Yes, follow your passion, but pack properly for the trip.

Objective/Summary

Let's talk objectives for your current project.

That's easy, right? What's an objective? It's what I want to have happen, right?

Let's look at a few examples:

- I want to build a better mousetrap.
- I want to write a book and sell a million copies.
- I want to write the next Harry Potter and be a billionaire.
- I want to develop a series of paintings that sell for $1,000 each.

What do you think?

I think they suck. Each of these is all about the person developing the idea, not the idea itself. Personal goals can be part of this, but not the focus. The focus should be on the project or the business and summarize the benefit I'm bringing to my target customer. No one cares if your project or your business helps you. They care about the benefit it brings to them.

Consider these:

- Develop a series of paintings inspired by Rainbow Row in Charleston, SC that can be developed as prints and signed originals. Targeted to residents of the greater Charleston, SC area and visitors wishing to take a piece of history with them.
- Develop a cost-effective casual shoe from molded plastics targeting casual beachwear, and other aquatic activity markets. (Think Crocs, and how those exploded).
- Develop a book series featuring a boy wizard going through childhood, puberty, and early adulthood to face the classic foe who killed his parents. Series to be targeted at kids to young adults. (Harry Potter)
- Develop a new physics-based game featuring Fowl vs. Swine, with potential pseudo educational aspects. Targeted for mobile and tablet devices on the Apple and Android platforms for users of all ages. Will be sold in the $.99 range vs. freemium models. (Angry Birds)

As you can tell, none of these are complex. You can develop the idea and overview as much as you need to, depending on your audience. If you develop the business plan for yourself to help keep yourself on track, this can be as generic or detailed as you need. If you're using the plan as part of your pitch to an agent, publisher, or someone funding your project, you may need to include a greater level of detail.

For larger projects, depending on how much you've planned, you may detail it a seven-book series, twenty paintings, etc.

You want your objectives to summarize the project, so you or anyone else who may need to look at your business plan can have a basic idea in a few minutes. You'd be shocked how quickly most people make decisions about whether or not to engage in a particular piece of work.

Think of this is as your elevator pitch. What would you say to your perfect customer or investor to hook them, if you only had ten seconds? And then once you have that, add detail assuming you've gotten their attention.

What good does this do me in my project plan?

- It gives you a quick reminder about the project if you haven't looked at it in a while.
- It gives interested parties enough information to decide if they want to go further.
- It gives a big picture definition of what you're doing, your target market, and even personal goals, if they are relevant.

Overview and Goals

Didn't we just finish defining objectives?

We did. So, what's this section for?

If the objective is your thirty second elevator pitch, this is your next step at the three-minute presentation. You're in the door, but your customer isn't sold. This is also where you may start working in your personal needs and goals in addition to the ones for the project.

This is also where you build your bigger business case for the project.

You'll want to include:

- Details about the project.
- High level timeline.
- High level budget
- Expected returns and time frame.
- What it delivers for your customers.
- Who are your customers/target market.
- What resources you require to complete the project.
- An overview of your company, team, or the people involved.

Consider this example:

Genre Publishing Company is developing an anthology book themed to take advantage of the current interest in Victorian England and the resurgence of interest in Sherlock Holmes. The anthology will feature twelve unique stories from one major author, five mid-level authors, and six unknown authors. Editing will be done by Hack and Slash Editing Services.

Each story is slated to be between six thousand to seventy-five hundred words, at six cents a word.

Overall budget for development is $8,000 with a total return of $10,000 over twelve months. Target price point is $17.99 retail, requiring 2,800 copies sold at retail to meet the goal.

Again, this is not a high level of detail and can include as much detail as you think you need, but in general expect three or four paragraphs, supported by details. This is just to help keep you, and anyone you partner with (such as other writers, editors, agents, etc.) in the same playbook.

The Business Cycle

Now that you have your first goal, you will find there are many cycles to business, just like in life. Basic operations are all about cycles. Daily, weekly, monthly, quarterly, annually. Pay bills. Send invoices. Do taxes.

Even larger is the cycle of bringing your work to life.

- Come up with an idea.
- Develop your strategy.
- Come up with a plan.
- Develop your product.
- Market to your customers.
- Deliver to your customers.
- Adjust and learn from what works and what doesn't.
- Rinse and repeat.

In any business, there's one really important factor: the ability to sell your product. I don't care if it's lattes, books, or Zumiez. Don't remember Microsoft's MP3 player? Neither did anyone else when they were trying to sell them. If you can't sell your product, you won't be in business for long.

Nor should you be.

There's another little surprise under the candy coating - just because it worked yesterday, doesn't mean it will tomorrow. Amazon and Facebook change on a regular basis, often to our frustrations. But there's a reason.

It helps them survive and thrive.

Depending on what your exact business model is, and your target audience, the success of any product is largely dependent on timing. Don't launch a cookbook for grilling in January. Do it in the spring when more people are ready to get outdoors. Your tax preparation guide had best be out January 1. Your Halloween story performs better in October than over Valentine's Day.

One final note about cycles. If your launch target for your book on having the perfect swimsuit body in May, your first draft had best be done in September. Meeting your release cycles will take longer than you think to have a quality product.

The Law of Unintended Consequences

As a final bit of preparation as you build your business, I want to share with you a little law I constantly strive to understand. I call it the Law of Unintended Consequences.

I do not want you to fear this law or treat it with a fatalistic view. You may be familiar with what is called Murphy's Law. It was named after Capt. Edward A. Murphy, an Air Force engineer. As a reference, you can see the history of what came to be known as Murphy's Laws (It is a long list) and all of the variations created over the years. (Take a look at **http://www.murphys-laws.com/** if you have a few spare hours some afternoon.) The short version boils down to "That which can go wrong, will, and at the least opportune time."

Having been a business and technology consultant for a long time, you learn to know, understand and love this adage. It motivates you to prepare and have contingencies. In many ways, I see this as another form of what I referred to earlier: resistance.

As a result, I have my own version I call the *Law of Unintended Consequences*. It can be neutral (though it rarely is.) Sometimes what looks like a crisis or disaster actually presents new options and opportunities. Often, unintended consequences are positive, such as a blog post going viral and bringing attention. Waiting in a long line at the coffee shop lets you connect with a new friend or business connection.

Things will rarely go exactly to plan, if ever. The important part of this critical law is to know it exists and watch for when it comes into effect. Be ready to deal with or take advantage of the consequences.

The universe rewards persistence, if you can earn it.

Defining Your Business

"Storytelling remains basic: It's just a campfire, the human connection that says you're not alone."
- Shonda Rhimes

The business of writing has changed a great deal since my first forays into it in the 1980's. I started on the journalism path, did some short stories, but mostly worked for clients. As I moved into my career, I did a great deal of business planning, project planning, and research. Today I do a mix of fiction and non-fiction writing, consulting in the business, working with speakers and presenters, and other consulting for corporate and entrepreneurial clients.

Having worked in technology for over twenty-five years, the digital revolution has touched all of our lives, and I've had the good fortune to be part of it. Like so many other industries, writing and publishing has undergone a transformation.

Being a business owner requires a different mindset than someone who has a career in a given field, working for others. We all work for someone, and hopefully it's our customers. This is a scary thought for most people. Most artists just want to create. Understanding all of the other pieces, and how the puzzle fits together, gives you the greatest opportunity for success.

Also, understanding all of the different areas making up the business gives you opportunities to explore ways of generating revenues and making a living in the business.

Traditional vs. Self-publishing

There is a fundamental difference between traditional publishing and self-publishing. One assumption I am going to make throughout this book is that at some point in your career, you are likely to self-publish some of your work. There are three career models for authors today:

- Traditionally published authors, whether through the large New York publishing houses or through mid-size and micro-presses, operate where the publisher buys the book and is responsible for paying all of the expenses related to development and production of the book. This includes editing, covers, etc. Traditional publishing operates under a principle called Yog's law. "Money flows toward the author."
- James D. Macdonald created Yog's Law in response to the rise in vanity publishers and their often-fraudulent business practices.

- Most traditional publishers require an agent for submission, though some smaller presses do not, or have open windows for submission to slush.
- Self-publishing is where the author takes on the role of both the author and the publisher. They are responsible for everything, including costs, quality, and publication.
- Hybrid publishing has become popular in recent years where authors publish both through publishing houses and self-publishing as well. In some cases, it is where self-published authors gain traditional publishing contracts after building a base. Other traditionally published authors take to self-publishing to release work that has not found a home in traditional publishing, or for work where they want creative control.
- Vanity publishing is a form of self-publishing. Vanity publishers are not publishing houses, but author services companies presenting themselves as publishers, often at high costs for the services provided.

No matter what path you take, the author is going to hold most, if not all of the responsibility for marketing their books.

If you're interested in learning more about your publishing options, come to **https://www.authoressentialsworkshops.com/** and the Paths to Publication workshop.

Life Cycle of a Book Project

No matter what you write, no matter the format, there is a life cycle to every piece of work Even a blog post has a similar cycle; it's just the duration and the total level of effort that can vary.

In the previous section, I talked about the business life cycle. Consider the writing process as the product life cycle.

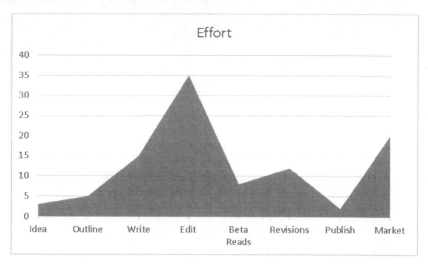

Most people assume writing is the majority of the effort. This is quite far from the truth. The biggest efforts will be in editing and revising your work. Over time, your skills will improve, and your first draft will be much cleaner as you stop making some time-consuming mistakes. Even so, plan to invest a lot of effort during the editing phase, even though much of it will be the work of others (your editors).

The Hierarchy of Needs

In 1943, psychologist Abraham Maslow came up with the Hierarchy of Needs. Since that time, it has been disputed, revised, expanded, and adapted. I look at it as a good tool for writers, artists and business people in general.

Hierarchy of Needs

You will find many variations of the Hierarchy of Needs since its initial development. I encourage researching it further based on your own specific requirements. It represents the personal growth from our most basic needs as a biological entity trying to survive, to fulfillment of our greater purpose.

As you satisfy your needs and build a foundation, new needs and desires emerge, moving you up the pyramid. As an individual, it is a useful tool in personal and professional growth and development.

As a writer, it is a useful tool for product development. For the fiction writer, it is the basis of character development and world building. It helps you create motivations, conflict, and realistic environments. For all other purposes, it defines the problems your product is intended to address and the solutions.

For your business, it lets us see how it has a life of its own and equips us to help it grow and mature.

Basic Needs

Starting at the bottom of the pyramid, Basic Needs are exactly that. The bare minimum we need to exist.

We start with biological imperatives. Without food, we die in weeks. Without water, we die in days. Without clothing and shelter, we can die in hours. Without air, we die in minutes. Beyond that, this tier covers our basest instincts for procreation, sleep, and the elimination of waste.

This applies to our business as well: without revenue and investment of resources, we have no business.

Once we have satisfied the minimum biological imperatives, we then look to address our most minimum physical safety requirements. We seek shelter from the elements and predation. We seek companionship as there is strength in numbers, and we can assist each other in times of need.

For your business, you cannot operate as an island. We depend on other individuals and businesses to survive.

Psychological Needs

Once the minimum imperative needs to survive are met, we move into the Psychological Needs. What is important is to remember, not only do you have these needs, so does everyone else on the planet. We interpret and manifest these needs in different ways. This also means we satisfy these needs according to their manifestation.

As an infant, one of the most important needs we have is for the love and care of our parents and immediate family. Without this, the effects can last a lifetime. As we move further into society, we built networks and communities.

The internet and social media enable us to find communities of shared interests like has never been possible in history. This is even true for businesses connecting with people. Alternately, it has also reduced or eliminated physical social contact and interaction for many people.

Self-esteem is the belief and recognition we each have value. Unless we each have self-respect, and regard for our talents and abilities, it is hard for anyone else to see or value us as well. Self-esteem also equips us to see and understand others for who they are, be they our friends and family, business partners, or customers.

As a business, if you do not believe in your own product, why would anyone else?

Cognitive Needs signify the point we cross over into our greater selves. This is the point we have the ability, and the luxury to pursue knowledge. It enables us to explore the world around us, question our purpose, and the meaning of life.

For our business, this is when we stretch the boundaries and find the problems and questions we wish to solve with our products.

Meeting the Aesthetic Need allows us to see and appreciate the beauty, and sometimes horror of the world around us. From the study of the microscopic to Hubble images of the universe, from language to math, we can explore and revel in being.

Your book covers, promotional artwork, your website, and even the language you use all ties into your final product, and attracts people to your work, and to you.

Self-Fulfillment Needs

Having addressed our Basic and Psychological Needs, we now have the tools and the ability to pursue our hopes and dreams by turning them into defined goals and ambitions.

Self-Actualization is the stage where we have matured into the process of identifying goals and actually meeting them. This is true both for us as individuals, and as business entities.

Not part of the original definition in 1943, Transcendence was the result of Maslow's continued study when he found those who achieved Self Actualization then pursued and achieved what he called the "peak experience." These are life changing moments when we are able to truly connect with something beyond ourselves. Whether moments of great love, bliss, or profound understanding, those achieving the capstone were able to transform not only themselves, but the world around them.

Hierarchy of Needs - Quick Reference

Type of Need	Need	The Individual	Business
Self-Fulfillment	Transcendence	Realization and using your complete being for the benefit of society	Thought and idea leadership, social responsibility.
	Self-Actualization	Realization of personal potentials	Personal and commercial success and recognition.
Psychological	Aesthetic Needs	Appreciation of the beauty and appearance of the world around us. Art, nature, symmetry and balance.	Market and brand presence and recognition.
	Cognitive Needs	Knowledge, understanding, curiosity, exploration, and need for meaning.	Resources for research, collaborative partners, beta readers.
	Esteem Needs	Self-esteem, and a respect for others.	Established tools, processes, methodologies for producing work.
	Belongingness and Love Needs	Giving and receiving love and affection, sense of community.	Relationships with customers and supporting partners, social media.
Basic	Safety Needs	Protection from potential physical and psychological dangers, including illness, the elements, and other risks.	Growth, profitability, marketing
	Biological and Psychological Needs	Need for food, air, water, rest, etc.	Working space, power, working capital.

The better you are able to understand yourself and your customers, the better able you are to reach and serve them.

The Writing Business

"No matter how small a project you work on, and no matter what it is, put your heart and soul and sense of responsibility into it."
- Frank Gehry

No matter your part in the creative process, whether you are an author, editor, cover or voice artist, or any of the other roles that bring creative work to life, you are part of the engine of the business. Most people in publishing are small businesses. Whether a company of one to a few dozen, everyone has a vested interest in the success of the business, even if they are not the owner/operator.

Calling our fans and readers customers is recognizing them for who they are. We want to recognize and be thankful for what they are to us as creators, but also what they mean to the survival and growth of our business. Customers are the lifeblood of business, and we have an opportunity to build that personal relationship by sharing our creative output.

Calling our work a product reminds us that the output of our creative selves is unique, but among thousands of other pieces of creative work. It is the result of turning our ideas, intellectual property, time and money into something others can appreciate.

I've seen and heard the phrase "authorpreneur" thrown around a lot in recent years. It's catchy, and gets some of the point across, but I think it also muddies the waters.

To me, the term stretches well beyond being within the writing and publishing business. As a term, it means you are writing and publishing as a part of your business, but it is only part of your business model.

For example, it can be "publish or perish" if you are in or want to be in any of these areas:

- Academia or research
- Thought or movement leading
- Niche expertise
- Speaking/talks/presentations
- Consulting
- Coaching
- Advising/mentoring

I am not being specific about the type of writing or publishing here. It is simply a fact that if you wish to get attention for yourself and the services you provide, making your thoughts and ideas available through modern media is critical.

Every business is a writing business, in some way.

For me, I write in a number of professional areas, mainly business and technology, but I also write fiction and produce entertainment content.

The ability to mentally separate the business side from the creative gives me the tools to detach from my work when I need honest feedback and critique, or when I need to evaluate it as a product, not the results of my chosen craft. I own a business, and the products and services are my intellectual property.

It can be hard to take an impersonal look at your creative output, but developing that skill is invaluable. It helps develop and grow your business as well as additional products and services.

I am a writer and a glass artist. I am also a business and technology consultant. I have integrated both of these parts of myself to build the different businesses I have and to advise my clients. In developing this program, I hope to give you the tools to be more successful than you dare to dream, and prepare you to handle the success.

This module is dedicated to the different types of businesses within the publishing industry, establishing a foundation for your business by building your platform, and other ways of making money through your craft.

Your Author Platform

The current buzzword for authors is to have your Author Platform. Much of this book will refer to specific pieces of your platform, and how to grow it, but what does this really mean? Why is it important?

Being a tech guy, I like the term "platform." It conveys a good idea for what you are doing with your business. To adapt a few of the common definitions a little bit, a platform is a raised structure that supports people or objects, a framework on which computer programs can run, or the principles and ideas of an organization.

My definition instead of Author Platform, think in terms of the Creator's Platform. So many facets of your business go beyond writing, and even the act of creating a book is greater than the written word. Most creative people I know express it in more than one way, be it writing, speaking, singing, acting, painting, sculpting, metalwork, jewelry design, and so much more.

With all this in mind, your platform is the set of tools and techniques used to raise the visibility of an individual, their work, and their brand to build a relationship of trust with existing and future fans and customers.

Unless you already are well known or are one of the few people with a large built in audience, your Platform will be all of the ways you build your market, and connect with people. As you make your way through this book, much of the focus will be on the parts of your Creator's Platform as the foundation for your business:

- Your website
- Creating content, including books, articles, blog posts, podcasts, videos, newsletters, digital downloads, etc.
- Social media
- Public speaking and media appearances
- Training classes
- Working with contacts, peers, influencers, and others to create and share content
- Working with groups, organizations and events relevant to your work

Not all of these may apply to you and your work, but it is good to have options as you grow. What is important is understanding what works best to communicate and develop relationships with your customers.

This looks like a lot of work, and in truth, it is. Your Platform will not be built in a day, and it will take time for your audience to find you. It is better to start small and build, than to overload yourself. And even if there are things you can do yourself, that does not mean you should do them all yourself. (That's one of which I'm often guilty)

Creators Creating

One of the key lessons as a business owner is learning how to delegate. You cannot do everything yourself, and though you may have the ability to do many of these tasks, you cannot do all of them well.

I am as guilty as many others (or more so) in that I have strengths and skills in these areas and do things I should hand off. I consciously decide (most of the time) which are important enough for me to do, and where I should invest my time versus having someone else get it done.

Some tasks require you hand them off. If you are a writer, you need editors. Period. You need beta readers. You need honest and critical feedback, or your marketplace will do it for you. You cannot step out of your mind and body to get the different eyes and opinions others can give.

You're on the path of turning your passion into your profession. Lovers love, haters hate, musicians play, and creators create. Creating for a living can be one of the most wonderful and rewarding ways of making your way in this world. It's still a business though, with all of the pitfalls, challenges, trials and tribulations. There are three key mindsets you will have at various points working in this business:

- **I am an artist, and I will create!** As an artist and a creator of work, whether it is the biography of Oliver Cromwell, a science textbook, or a thriller, there are creative aspects. As a business, this is the amateur mindset.
- **It's a job.** I sit down during my prescribed times and crank out the material. When my day is done, I will take care of the rest of life. This is the professional mindset.
- **I am dedicated to my success.** I will live by the mantra; Only do the work that only you can do. I will plan and understand my business, my customers, and my marketplace. I will hire people for their skills. I will ensure that I give my customers the products they expect and deserve, and they will support me in return. This is the business owner.

There's a dirty little secret: you are likely to shift between these mindsets, depending on the project and what else is happening in your life.

When you find yourself slipping backwards, ask yourself: is your time better spent designing a web page, cleaning house, or putting out your next book? There are only so many hours in a day, and sleep is going to get some of them. So are family, friends, your day job if you have one (and many writers do).

In this section, we'll look at the good, the bad and the ugly, as well as the realities of writing and publishing as a profession and a business by looking at the various people and functions you will either do, or work with.

As you read this book, remember: you are your own most valuable asset and resource. Spend it wisely.

Up the Revenue Stream Without a Paddle

Maybe the light bulb came on for you and you cranked out a short story in a weekend. Maybe it is the result of years of research and work.

Congratulations!

You have your product and are ready to rake in the cash. Or at least we're going to assume you do for this section.

Guess what? The easy part is over.

Unless you were contracted to develop the piece of work, now you need to see about selling it. Hopefully, you gave this consideration before you started, or worst case you are thinking about it now that you have this book.

There are many things to consider at this point, and more every day as new options in publishing and other sources of revenue are created. You are going to find that many of the answers depend on you individually, your skill sets, and the various tasks you are willing and able to do yourself.

Beyond that, what can you do with the work and monetize it? For building your brand? To generate extra revenue?

Whether you develop content as your primary business, or if it is one part of your overall business strategy, two key ideas that will propel you forward are the "synergy of ideas" and "re-purposing of content." These two ideas go hand in hand.

The synergy of ideas is developing and sharing common ideas or themes through a particular program or body of work in such a way that the whole is greater than the sum of its parts. For example, Chicken Soup for the Soul has grown from a single book to an empire, but the common theme is taking personal stories and experience in uplifting and enlightening ways regardless of the theme or premise. It is just as true for a book about people's spiritual beliefs or cat themed coloring books. For this book, it is business strategy through the language of creativity.

Re-purposing of content creates and reinforces consistency in your message, saving you time and effort. For example, imagine you have a book like this, and then used excerpts as blog posts and narration on your podcast. You would be delivering the same message to your customers in multiple ways.

Using these concepts, how many ways can you use your creative products? We'll dive deeper in **Revenues (Got to get Paid!)**.

What Kind of Writer are You, and What Kind Do You Want to Be?

What kind of writer are you, and what kind do you want to be?

A common start in the industry is writing or editing within an organization and developing content specific to their needs. Best known are those working in journalism and academics. Also common are developing press releases, training materials or manuals.

Others get their start or develop their careers as a freelance writer. This means you are an independent contractor developing content either for yourself or others. You will likely move into many of these models as you progress through your career:

There are a lot of ways you can explore and grow your business:

- The "traditional" path of writing full-length books, novels and novellas, whether fiction or non-fiction, be it memoirs, biopics, or thrillers.

- Contractual ghost writing that both generates revenues and develops your skills under someone else's name.
- Freelance journalism involves researching and developing stories for printed and online periodicals and journals, depending on your experience and expertise.
- Development of professional materials. This may include documentation, training and educational materials, or presentations for others in technical or procedural applications.
- Blogging blends generating revenues and brand building, allowing you to reach potentially huge numbers of people. Quite a few people make a living purely from their blogs. It also allows you to hone your skills while you talk about the things you have expertise in, know and love.
- Screen writing for film or stage.
- Copy-writing is specialized writing for marketing and advertising.
- Researching material and developing content outlines for other writers.
- Becoming an editor, both generating revenue and giving you valuable skills.

The tools, technologies, and industry have grown to support self-published authors in a way not imaginable ten years ago. Within seconds of finishing a blog post or article, they can be available online. A book can be available for sale in under twenty-four hours.

As emphasized throughout this book, the ability to publish this way carries no guarantee of content or quality. Nor does it guarantee anyone will ever see or read it.

For many, the goal is to be traditionally published through medium and large presses. For others it's a career in media or marketing agency. Building skills and creating your personal network is key to success no matter what you want.

In the modern publishing world, the vast majority of people who publish for large presses are now hybrid authors. This means they are doing a mix of publishing through the medium and large houses but are also publishing independently and through smaller houses as well. The benefit of having a large-scale house publishing your work gives you exposure and credibility. Small-press and self-publishing give you freedom to develop less commercial work, or simply work you want to get to your fans quickly. I've even known authors to use this path to complete series dropped by their publishers. For others, it's their path to New York publishing.

As described in Creators Creating, writers also often offer editorial services. This helps both you as a writer and your customers. Developing your editorial skills can only help you in your craft and provide service to your fellow creators.

You are your business, and your brand. Own it. Be what you want others to read and buy. They are your customers. Explore all of the avenues open to you.

Education and Development Writing

As a creator, if you have certain areas of expertise or can work with experts, there is great demand and value developing and publishing training, educational, and informational programs for individuals and institutions.

As internet security is a major concern for businesses large and small, a program could include:

- On-demand training videos
- Books/presentations
- Forums restricted to the member base
- Social media groups for member base networking
- Podcast/audio training
- Live training

Either individually or part of a larger team, you can deliver specialized material using multimedia options to consumers of the material.

Applications and Games Authors

The explosion of digital technology, especially in tablets and smartphones, has created a new market and delivery method for interacting with people. Whether you are a career counselor or a science fiction writer, there are ways to develop your material into a game or service application. You will also find writers are the backbone of traditional and digital entertainment such as trivia and role-playing games.

I've Got My Product, What Now?

"A good novel tells us the truth about its hero; but a bad novel tells us the truth about its author."
- *Gilbert K. Chesterton*

All of us that regularly use computers or do anything online have experienced when a patch is released by Microsoft or Apple, or Facebook changes how it works. Frequently, a new product or feature is bare bones when it's rolled out, and the bells and whistles come later, if it survives long enough. This is a philosophy known as "minimum viable product."

As an author, if you are releasing a book, this is a philosophy you cannot afford. The work you publish needs to be the best quality you can release. We rarely get a second opportunity to introduce readers to an author they didn't like the first time.

Before you panic, no book is perfect. Even the best vetted New York Times bestseller has typos. There are always opportunities to improve. That's why you see second, third, and fourth editions. This isn't what I'm talking about.

If you are going through a traditional publisher, they will be a big part of the process to bring a quality book to market. However, if you are self-publishing or trying to get an agent or book deal, the book you are delivering needs to meet the level of quality for which you want to be known.

Typing "The End" is just the first step in this journey, followed by editing, beta reads, and rewrites. [If you have not yet completed your first round of edits and rewrites, gotten impartial feedback, and polished your work, you are not ready to move to the next step. Make your work the best it can be first.]

Before you started on your project, hopefully you had some idea of who would be interested in buying or reading it. Maybe you started down one path, and the story went another. No matter how you get there, once you have a product, you need to figure out who will want it. This is much harder when you are first starting out than once you have some experience. Let's assume you have written a book you want to publish and sell and have done nothing else. Today, you have more options than ever to get it published.

Dig deep and consider your long-term career goals. As an author, there are three options for publishing of your book:

- *New York Publishing, or the Big 5*, are the large presses and their numbers of different imprints used for publication, depending on genre and author. These are the old guard of traditional publishing, and for many authors, a symbol of success and recognition. Agents are required to submit in this space.
- *Small Press Publishing* has blossomed in the digital age, in no small part due to the technological innovations in ebooks and Print on Demand services giving the infrastructure of larger presses with minimal investment. Small presses open up traditional publication to a wider spectrum of authors. Depending on the publisher, an agent may or may not be required.
- *Self-publishing* puts the author in the position of being both the author and the publisher. This also means the author is responsible for all decisions and financial investments.

No matter if you are going to try and land an agent, sell to a publisher, or do it yourself, there is the all-important question: who would want to buy it, and why?

Unless you intend to self-publish, the next step is submitting your manuscript to an agent or publisher. Do your research to determine if they represent or publish your genre of work, and no matter what, *read and follow the submissions guidelines.*

The inquiry and submission process is fundamentally the same for agents or directly to the publisher (if they accept direct submissions). There are professional standards you can expect to follow:

Make sure your work is polished and ready for prime time. It is better to have your work professionally critiqued, and I'm talking about a circle larger than friends and family. Make sure your work is ready for a commercial market. Know how to write well, and with a commercial viewpoint. You have a personal investment in the work, and someone who does not can give you honest and sometimes brutal critique before it comes from others in the business, or your readers. It is better to have feedback before pursuing publication.

Follow the guidelines of each person or organization where you submit your work. (This really is a good contender for rule number one, but exists here for a reason.) There are standards in the industry, such as submitting in Times New Roman font, 12-point font size. If a publisher asks for 78-point Comic Sans, send it in 78-point Comic Sans. Following the guidelines is an easy way for a publisher to judge your level of professionalism. Not following directions is an easy way to have your work dismissed without even the most cursory review. Agents and editors are looking for any reason to trim down their slush pile versus looking for the next great story. Do not send your great romance novel to someone who publishes technical journals. If someone asks for the first five pages, do not send a thousand-page manuscript. If someone asks for highlighting adverbs in lime green, do it.

Expect rejection. Learn to know and love rejection letters. Paper your walls with them. For those that personalize the rejection, take their feedback to heart. If someone has taken the time to give feedback instead of a generic rejection letter, use it as a learning experience. And when you think you cannot take another rejection, keep writing and send it out again.

Learn when a piece is not worth submission. If the feedback tells you your work is not ready, take it to heart. It will be up to you to decide if the work can be saved, or if it is time to set it aside and produce something new. It can be hard, but you cannot take it personally. This is business.

Write a great cover letter. Personalize it for every submission. If you have any connection with the person or organization, put it in the cover letter so they have a little more of a reason to give you a look. Otherwise, keep it short, sweet and professional.

Perfect your elevator pitch. Be able to describe your work in one hundred words or less, preferably less than twenty.

Be professional, most of all. You have a business, the publisher has a business, the agent has a business, and you need to consider any transactions as being business to business. Yes, you have poured your heart and soul into your work, but at this level, it is one product among many. You need to have or at least understand the independent and critical eye the industry takes to all work, not just yours.

What else can you do to improve your chances of getting your work accepted for publication?

- Network. Connect with other authors, editors, and industry people. When you are starting out, it is much harder to build connections and relationships. There are many events all over the country and throughout the year where agents interview large numbers of authors, evaluate submissions, and speak about the industry. Like any business, relationships are key, and help you build more.

- Write more. Just because one work does not sell or draw the attention you are looking for, keep writing. At worst, you are developing and honing your skills.
- As with anything, the internet can be really useful. Do your research on anyone you are looking to do business with. The more effort you put in on the front end, the better equipped and more likely you are to have a successful outcome.
- And most importantly, be resilient.

Author Essentials offers the online "Path to Publication" workshop diving deeper into all of this and more.
(https://www.authoressentialsworkshops.com/)

Vanity, begone.

You may have also heard of something called "vanity presses" or "vanity publishers." These companies are not publishers, but are publishing services companies, and you are in essence expensive self-publishing. I cannot recommend using a vanity publisher, as they tend to charge premium prices for the services they offer, and often make promises that they cannot keep. In my opinion, if you see the words "vanity press," do not pass go, and do not give them $200, even in Monopoly money. If you have a few minutes, look into the book project Atlanta Nights, a project done to expose vanity presses. (Start with https://en.wikipedia.org/wiki/Atlanta_Nights)

Rejection

Ever tried. Ever failed. No matter. Try again. Fail again. Fail better.
- Samuel Beckett

There's an old adage. "In life there's only two certainties: death and taxes." As a writer there's a third. Rejection.

Rejection isn't always bad. It doesn't mean your work isn't good. Rejection may come because your work didn't meet the current market conditions, or the criteria of the person to whom you submitted. If you receive something more than a standard form rejection, take the feedback to heart.

To understand this part of the business, whether your work was submitted to an agent, a publisher, or even a request for a personal appearance, there's no guarantee of acceptance, but there are a lot of ways to ensure sure you aren't accepted.

- *You don't follow the guidelines.* The easiest way to make sure you don't even get a first look is to ignore the guidelines. You may do your drafts in a rainbow of colors in eighty-seven-point wingdings. Do not send it to anyone else that way.

  For submission guidelines, there are a few standards that most people go by. Twelve point, Times New Roman in black in a .doc format is usually the standard. Do your research about margins, page numbering, footnotes, line spacing, etc, and understand guidelines will differ by agent and publisher.

- *Include a professional cover page* with your name, your contact information,

  Cover the basics, who you are, contact information, your publishing resume, your agent (if you have one), your title (even though it may change), the genre and word count, and a concise summary. Do not include your life story, unless it is relevant to the book (such as in a memoir).

- *Your tone or attitude.* This is a business. If your attitude appears unprofessional, or you seem to be difficult to work with, even the best manuscript can be rejected. Present yourself as someone people want to do business with.

- *Your manuscript doesn't fit the agent or the publisher.* If your manuscript is a cookbook and you submit it to someone who is in the professional development market, it likely won't make it past the cover letter.

- *Your writing needs improvement.* Be honest with yourself. Ask someone else to read your work with a critical eye, and give you an impartial critique. Is your language too flowery? Are your characters straight from the stockroom? Is your story original? Is it boring? Is it good, just not ready for prime time? Does your story just suck? Enough said.

By no means are these the only reasons a story gets rejected. Submitting work is like walking in a minefield. It may not even be anything you did. Editors, agents and slush readers are people too, having their own tastes, reactions to subjects and topics, and pet peeves that can lead to rejection. One bad step, and into the rejection pile you go. They may even be having a bad day. Ensure you present your best self and best work where you have the most influence and control.

So, remember, when you are asking people to look at you and your work, give them positive reasons to do so. Most agents, editors, and people reviewing the slush pile have more in front of them than you can imagine, work long hours, and often for little pay. To you, yes, your work is special. To them, it's one more piece to slog through, hoping to find a gem to be worth picking up and compelling to read just one more line.

3: Sales and Marketing

Sales vs. Marketing

"The aim of marketing is to know and understand the customer so well the product or service fits him and sells itself."
- Peter F. Drucker

It may seem a little obvious, but if no one is buying, you won't be in business long. If you have been around business for any length of time, you usually hear sales and marketing grouped together as if they were one entity and job.

While interconnected, sales and marketing are two separate business functions with a similar objective: to increase revenues. For those of us in small business, the process can often be painful and humiliating while we look for return on the other end.

Without sales, you do not have a business. Without marketing, you aren't going to sell much.

How are sales and marketing different?

Sales targets the short term and is the process of focusing on small specific groups or individuals with the intention of converting their wants and needs into demand for your products.

Marketing studies the long game of developing your brand, creating awareness of your existence with potential customer bases, and understanding what your potential customers want.

We often see this process depicted as a funnel:

One of the big points to notice, happy readers feed back into your marketing funnel. Satisfied customers and readers are your best evangelists, because word of mouth is still king!

As an author, unless you are one of the top performers for a given publisher, you are largely responsible for marketing and advertising. As you consider your marketing plan and put it into action, remember one of the key lessons of being a writer: Show don't tell. Make your reader feel throughout the process.

How you do this is by creating great content, developing an integrated brand, and by being professional. As a creative person and creator of content, people want to feel like they have some degree of relationship with you.

This is also one of the areas your agent can assist, but beyond whatever marketing and advertising your publisher provides, the rest (the majority) will fall to you. A publicist specializes in getting you in front of audiences and coaching you on approach and style. While they will help, often drive the planning phase and use their network to create opportunities, they should be the backbone of executing the plan.

A few tips:

- You will not always know what parts of your plan are working and which ones are not. Paid advertising can give you good metrics on click through and purchases. Bookmarks and SWAG are more indirect.

- Invest enough in your marketing efforts to give them time to work. A one-day campaign will rarely be enough to tell if something is working.

- If, after a reasonable period of time, something is not working, do not be afraid to change or stop it and try something else.

- When you make changes to a campaign, do them incrementally. If you make too many changes at once, you may not be able to determine which change was effective (such as changing images, your targeted customers, and the title for the campaign).

- You will have to invest in owned media, earned media, and paid media (we will explore these in depth later) to rise above the noise in your markets. These investments are not only for the short-term sale but the long-term relationship with your readers and customers.

- Especially leading up to and during a launch, plan to be more active on social media and engaging all of your contacts through earned media.

- Use and reward your true fans and true customers. They will be the first ones to buy your products and share the good word. Take care of them and find ways to reward them for supporting you (SWAG for instance). It's easier to sell an existing customer than find a new one.

Let's Get Digital (Marketing)

Depending on your viewpoint, the digital age began somewhere between the 1950's and 1970's, but the real transition took hold in the 1980's. The first major public gateway onto the internet was Compuserve Information Service (also known as CIS or just Compuserve.)

Growing out of several short-lived Internet Service Providers (ISP's) in the 1980's, America OnLine (or AOL) dominated the 1990's with its native browser, email, chat and other applications.

Since then, having an online presence has gone from being a novelty to a near necessity. This could not be truer for those in publishing, of those who wish to have their work known, or even available.

The great news about the digital frontier is that we now live in a time of "internet famous." People build careers and businesses simply out of being themselves online. Technology allows us to distribute product in almost any media to the public instantaneously. It even allows one-person businesses access to the global marketplace. We have even seen these one-person businesses become global powerhouses (ex. Amazon).

The down side? You are swimming upstream against everyone else. Sometimes it's the one thing you do not want known or one stupid mistake that "goes viral" and brings fame in a way you never wanted.

Does this mean not to try? Hell no!

You are a creator and a businessperson. You have art and a commercial product. Treat it like such and be professional. You are going to make mistakes, and that's great. You may even luck into one of Bob Ross' "happy accidents." The world of social media thrives on showing people at their best, and their worst. Always show your best self, but a few warts remind everyone your human and makes it easier to connect.

As you move into the digital world, everything can be classified as one of the following:

- Owned media is any content you have control and is part of your brand. This includes your hosted website, mailing list, podcasts, white papers, etc. You can extend the influence of your owned media through social media and sites such as Amazon and Goodreads through posting an author profile. While these are part of your owned media and are valuable, you are subject to their standards, structures, and content requirements.

  The importance of owned media is your ability to create and deliver your exclusive content and compose the framework of your brand, your way. Outside of the structures and limitations of the platforms you use(and applicable laws), you have complete control.

- Earned media is exposure you cultivate through word-of-mouth and organic growth (new leads and sales generated by your internal processes and existing fans and customers). This is generated through positive reviews, social media share, blog shares and reposts, SEO content, and publicity from mentions in media, through events, peers, and fans.

  Earned media builds interest and trust with those who visit your owned media by transferring some of the credibility of the sources onto you.

- Paid media is funded promotion such as advertising in traditional and social media and sponsorship of events. Paid media is most beneficial with "warm" traffic (people who have some awareness of your work), when cultivating earned media, and when you have special events such as product launches to drive traffic to your owned media. Paid media draws attention to you with people who have never heard of you, but it takes longer and costs more.

The Marketing Triad

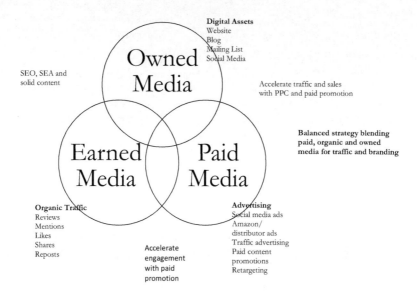

Where different types of media overlap, there are opportunities to gain more from blending properties. For example, where owned media and earned media overlap, it boosts the power of SEO (Search Engine Optimization), SEA (Search Engine Advertising) and solid content to driving traffic to your website, encouraging people to join your mailing list and engaging on social media.

Where paid media intersects earned and owned media, it boosts the value of every dollar spent by increasing brand awareness and giving the customer more ways and reasons to engage with you when they find valuable content. Paid advertising can only put you in front of potential customers, you still have to give them a reason to stay.

The critical part is having quality content you expose to your audience. Ideally, you find the balance point where paid content is exposing you to new customers, and who find your quality content, and other readers with which to engage.

Defining Your Market

"All of your marketing materials, such as your website, back cover copy, personal bio, bookmarks, newsletters, and even social media posts should explain how you can improve a reader's life."
- Rob Eagar

It may seem an odd question, but what does an author sell?

You immediately jumped up and said, "Books!" Am I right? Or something along those lines. If you did, you would be wrong.

You are selling your research, education and skills focused through the time spent practicing and honing your craft, packaged with countless hours of blood, sweat and tears to give your customer an experience, and pass on some part of yourself.

A little different, isn't it?

A few hundred years ago, books were seen as one of the most valuable assets one could own. Each was hand crafted and represented years of work just in the act of scribing it. The printing press was a revolution, making the written word available to the masses. Literacy was understood to be the gift and right to knowledge.

The digital age has brought a new revolution, making nearly anything available with the touch of a screen, but in a way, we have traded some of the reverence for the written word. As an author, it is your job and duty to preserve this idea and infuse it into everything you do. This will bring you your true fans; the people who love and respect you and your work.

If you value it, your readers will too.

Understanding the Marketplace

The marketplace is the backbone of business. It is not only where commerce happens, it defines the rules of the game from idea to product delivery.

It was not that many years ago where a person wanting to make a living as a writer only had a few choices. You worked in media, pursued a contract with one of the major publishers, worked in some business environment, or freelanced wherever you could take a gig. Then the digital revolution arrived, throwing the marketplace into an ever-evolving process.

We see the largest brick and mortar bookstore chains falling to the wayside, yet many independent bookstores are seeing a resurgence, despite Amazon's control of the market. Audiobooks now represent a material portion of all books read, being 25% of all electronic sales in 2017 at 2.5 billion and growing. Most people now have an electronic reader easily at hand, be it a computer, tablet, or phone.

These changes have also affected the way we reach potential readers.

As an example, the innovation of ebooks, and independent/self-publishing becoming 50% or more of book sales in some genres has opened up not only careers, but also product lines that would have never been published before. You can carry an entire library of resources on your hip. Or discretely read your guilty pleasure on the train without judgement from other passengers.

This also means the marketplace can change rapidly for businesses dependent on the it. Amazon's policy changes often affect independent authors, but they have also significantly influenced even the largest publishers. Following and understanding changes in the marketplace is necessary for success, to take advantage of new developments, technologies, and to guard against changes impacting you, your business, and how you interact with your customers.

Here's the good news… books and other media products are a lot more like consumables - cup of coffee or a sandwich than other types of merchandise. The act of buying one does not lock the customer into having the same thing every day, or even from the same place. And people's tastes change over time.

Unlike other types of sales, someone buying a book or product from a competitor can be a benefit. This is why Amazon has the "Frequently Bought With" and "Customers Who Bought X Also Bought" areas on their website.

If someone has an interest in a topic or genre, they will usually buy more than one book, video, or other product. If someone is trying to learn about sales mindset, they will usually read multiple books and authors. If you can't wait for your next James Patterson thriller, they buy something in the genre from another author. Today's reader's landscape is defined not only by the paperback in their hand, but the digital products on their phones and tablets. Customers enter bookstores and attend events for the experience, as any of these products are available online and shipped directly to their door.

What's next? The next phase of digital will likely be some socially acceptable form of Google Glass where the image is projected onto glasses, or even directly into the eyeball. Text to voice technology will approach that of conversant human voice. Even full multimedia and augmented reality experiences comparable to *Star Trek's* "holodeck" is on the horizon. Imagine the consumer not only reading but immersing themselves into a book full of music, sound effects, imagery, sights, and even smells.

Augmented and virtual realities will offer reading a book set on Mount Kilimanjaro surrounded by the appearance of an African savannah, or a book about writing taught to you by Stephen King. As authors, we may have to change to take the best advantage of these technologies, and what our fans want as an end product.

To break into or grow within a market, it is critical to know and understand it. This means understanding who your customers are, and who else is trying to fill their wants and needs. For a lot of products, it is win or lose. Think about buying a car or appliance. You are only going to do it so often.

Exercise:

1. Take a sampling of similar books currently in the market. Pick six to ten to start. Go to your local bookstore to look at the new releases and look at the top ten lists on Amazon.
2. Study the pricing and marketing strategies used by the publisher and the author, such as the titles, covers, and descriptions.
3. Read it for style and content.
4. Do market research to see how well it is, or is not, performing in the marketplace.

There is a big write-to-market movement in the ebook space. I am not a fan of it, because it mostly produces quickly-written, poorly-edited books chasing a fad. You can tell the author doesn't care about the subject and grabbing a quick buck from the hot topic of the day.

There are people that do it well, and there are times it's appropriate to chase a topical issue. Trying to rush out a crypto-currency book after listening to a few podcasts, or rushing a new superhero book out to capitalize on a trend rarely works, and can be harmful. It's the people with knowledge and expertise or who already have a track record in the genre that are best able to capitalize.

A long career in developing and publishing requires having some understanding of your markets, and what makes good business sense. If you write space operas, zombie books, and paranormal romance, know the trends in the genres, and whether the market is active. If you write diet and health related books, be able to respond to the fads. Every genre is cyclical, either in the popularity or trending topics.

I don't believe my fellow authors are competition. I can never write enough books or fast enough with even a moderate reader. And no reader wants to have the same thing for dinner every day, or read the same book over, and over again. Variety is the spice of life.

So how can you do market research?

There are a lot of tools available. Some are free or have a free version, and many are not. Often, you can try one out, but will have to pay for advanced features. (They are a business too.)

Once you have done your research, you can elect to write and publish books that won't sell if the market isn't there, hold onto the manuscripts until the right time, or you can tailor your work to where you believe the market is going. When authors collaborate in their markets, or at least cross promote, it makes the whole market stronger. This leads to understanding who else is writing successfully in your market.

Target Your Market

"Even when you are marketing to your entire audience or customer base, you are still simply speaking to a single human at any given time." – Ann Handley

In the last section, we explored how to study and understand the marketplace and where you wish to do business. To take it to the next step, we must understand who are the consumers in your marketplace and how to connect with them.

It's time to define your product ecosystem. That's a nice way of learning to define and understand:

- Who are my target customers?
- Where do I find them?
- What do they like?
- What do they want or need?
- How do they want to buy my product?
- How do they want it delivered?
- Who are the leaders in my market?
- Who else is in your market?
- Are there others in my market I can partner with?
- Who and how can assist me in delivering my product?
- How are others in my market advertising and marketing themselves and their products?
- What is in my control, and what isn't?
- What is not in my target market, even though it looks like it might be?

Depending on your art and your medium, you can have great differences in your environment. Let's consider jewelry artists for a moment. Think about being at an event where there are five different artists. Each has a different style, different products, and even different price ranges. If someone comes in with a fixed amount of money or looking for something for a particular purpose or style, those jewelers are each individually competing for that person and their dollars.

This is one of those times where writers and musicians can be a little different.

- Price points tend to be lower.
- No matter how much a writer produces, their readers can always read faster than the work can be produced.

- Partnering up can be of a greater benefit, by sharing with authors in comparable genres, you can help potential fans find new works and creators without hurting themselves. You have probably seen "If you like X, you'll love to get your hands-on Y." In fact, often by working together, the community and overall sales are stronger in the short and long terms for everyone.

- Everyone has different tastes, and people tend to look for art to help manage their moods, and to inspire them. Think about what you want for dinner. Even if it's your favorite food, you probably don't want it every night. Just because I'm in the mood for geeky vampires today doesn't mean I won't want or need a spy thriller tomorrow. While I drive to work, I may want classical to keep me calm and focused while I drive, and to get me ready for my day, and Ozzy on the way home Friday afternoon to get me ready for the weekend.

Let's go with the assumption your idea is for a non-fiction novel examining the future of medical technology. Here are the first questions I'll have:

- Who am I targeting? Is this for technologists to inspire them to build devices? Is it for mass market for those interested in futurism? Though you will have some crossover, these are two different audiences with two different purposes. It's also two different books.

- With the assumption you are doing one for more general readers, what do they want to see? If your primary livelihood is in a medical technology think tank, you might write this based on your own work and the work of your peers. If you're a reporter with no specific knowledge, you may be going around and interviewing people in the field to publish a series of essays, or interviews.

- Who else is writing similar material? Understanding competitors helps you better understand your overall market and customers. You're not Coke fighting Pepsi for the same beverage sale. And probably a whole lot better for the health of your customers, or at the minimum won't cause diabetes. Look at who is producing material in the same genre to see what they are producing, and how it's being received.

You may be asking yourself, how do I go about all this? It sounds like work.

It is work. You have a business, and you are a brand. To produce work you're happy to label with your name and your brand:

- *Read.* A lot. Both in and out of your field and genre. Stephen King said, "*If you don't have time to read, you don't have time to write.*" Reading non-fiction will tell you more about the human condition, and how the world works, in addition to informing you about the people and events within it. It is great inspiration, and education about your market. Read fiction outside of your genre. All genres have their formulas and tropes. Mix it up. Make your world realistic. Know the expectations of your readers and your genre so you can subvert and surpass them.

- *Listen to music.* I don't care what type of artist you are, music is a fantastic source of inspiration. It can enhance your moods and open you to powerful emotions. Exploring other forms of creativity influences and enhances your own.

- *Talk to people.* For that piece of non-fiction, even if it's something from your core world as a scientist, a technician, or entrepreneur, you need to exchange ideas with others in your field. No matter what, you'll never keep up with everything in our rapidly changing world. And discussion helps shape your own ideas.

- *The internet.* For most of us, this has become the go-to source for all knowledge. It is a fantastic tool, but recognize it for what it is. A tool. If nothing else, chasing an idea around various websites and publications will help you hone your BS meter. Be a journalist and use multiple reliable sources when you need facts. Watch and see how different sources will report the same story. It's also a great resource for finding individuals and groups with whom to talk, share ideas, and do research.

- *Visit specific organizations and their websites.* You were just talking about the internet and you're still doing it? Not exactly. If you're doing market research about who buys books on furniture restoration, there are companies that aggregate this data and provide other marketing services. Since Amazon is the 800-pound gorilla for so many ventures these days, do your research using their various services and tools, and others that interface with them (keyword engines, for example). Never rely on a singular source.

Look for people's experiences and how they handle them. Amazon continually works to provide the best experience for their (and our) customers. From personal experience, while Amazon provides a lot of fantastic services for authors, they also can be draconian and heavy-handed when they respond to problems with those vending through their platform. People who game the system trigger changes in the platform for short-term gain, and often create collateral damage to others in the process. For example, KDP Select is based on the number of pages read. People placed the table of contents for their books in the back and linked to it on the front page. Click on the link, and voilà, Amazon thinks you've read the whole book. As a result, if you have a book on KDP select, your TOC has to be in the front, or it will be pulled. Many legitimate authors had their titles pulled until they reformatted their ebooks because of having an index in the back.

Another reason continuous monitoring and adjustment to your market is critical is that they always are in a state of flux. Travel guides used to be popular frequently updated and released. For a certain block of authors, it was a good living, and you were paid to travel! Not long ago, I talked to someone who'd been a traveling reporter, but also produced guides from his experience and made quite a good side income until the mid to late 2000's. When the Internet became common, no one needed to buy guides anymore; all of the info was available online for free. If you have a question, a quick Google search on your smartphone give you all the info you need. Complete websites are dedicated to helping you build your trip. He still writes about travel, but now it goes to these sites. The model for his side business changed from full form books and guides to contributing to travel sites with articles and pictures.

Know your business and how it changes, or you'll spend a lot of time on a product you can't sell. The more time you invest in this process, even if your work is already written, or the picture is complete, the better your roadmap for getting your work out there.

Your Marketing Plan

"Content builds relationships. Relationships are built on trust. Trust drives revenue."
— Andrew Davis

The Marketing Plan merges all of the customer-impacting parts of your business plan and consolidates them in one singular view. It details your strategy for raising awareness, boosting you into the limelight so that people know about you and your work. Keep in mind as you build your brand, everything that you do or that a customer may see or interact with is part of your marketing effort.

One of the most common questions in business is "So what is the difference between marketing and advertising? Aren't they the same thing?"

Whether you are a one-person business or an international conglomerate, the answer is no.

Marketing is the strategy by which you plan to raise awareness, promote your brand and your products. Your marketing plan details who your ideal customer is, where they are, and the best ways to reach them. It understands what pricing your market will bear. It tells how you will ultimately put your product or service in the hands of your customers.

Advertising is the active part of your marketing plan where you engage with your customers through all of your media channels. It could be your e-mail list, social media, paid advertisements, or making appearances.

The easiest way to look at it, marketing is the overall strategy for branding you, your work, and the themes you use for particular books and products. Advertising is taking those themes, and actively using your chosen media to promote your materials.

Your Marketing Plan should pull together everything related to branding, raising awareness, and fulfillment. As you move into the planning phase and look at all of these pieces, you should ask yourself each of these questions for each step or task:

- *Is it simple?* If you come up with a large and complex plan, there are more pieces to break or fall through the cracks.
- *Is it Achievable?* If you put it in the plan, you need to be ready and able to do it. If you think something is a good idea, but cannot afford the investment of time or cost, reconsider it.
- *Is it Meaningful and purposeful?* Just because something can be done, make sure you should. For every component you add to your plan, ask yourself if it moves your plan along? Is it relevant to you? Much like writing fiction, if the effort does not materially move your plan along, it probably needs to be cut.

- *Is it consistent?* You should make sure any action you take fits you, your brand, and your overall strategy. If your message is all over the place, it's much harder for people to get to know you and what you want people to understand about you and your product.
- *Is it true to you?* Often, we see things that work well for others, or get suggestions on new ways to build our brand, and increase our visibility. Before investing time and resources into integrating an idea, make sure it resonates with you, your customers, and your fans. You are your brand. Be true to yourself.

With these ideas in mind, your plan should look something like this:
1. The Overview/Summary highlights your overall goals, strategy, and approach.
2. Your Target Market breaks information down to a detailed profile of your ideal customer(s). This would include:
   a. Demographics information, including age, gender, economic status, etc.
   b. Is there a specific location or region where most of your potential customers would be? For example, if you write about the history of a state, most of your reader base is probably in that region.
   c. What are the beliefs and values of your ideal customer? If you write about entrepreneurship, self-reliance and financial independence will be high priorities.
   d. What triggers their emotional and intellectual interest? Are your readers looking for ways to educate children along the autistic spectrum?
   e. Are there specific habits or behaviors? If you are writing a self-help series, who are the specific people you want to help? What is the problem or issue you want to fix?
3. The Customer Segment takes different elements, groups them by the common factors, details the common elements/factors, to develop your ideal reader profile. This is your Customer Avatar.
4. Your Competitor Comparison is your list of people and work you use as a measure of your work. Understanding your competitors also helps your readers and customers understand you, your products and services. An example would be the "also bought" list on Amazon.

5. Your Market Survey evaluates trends in your genre or space. Everything goes in cycles. Often, if a market is already hot, it is too late to jump in. You need to understand what is just bubbling to the surface. As a part of your survey, use the others in your market to compare your audiences and demographics. One of the biggest providers of independent reports for authors is k-lytics.com that specifically analyzes Kindle sales. Other ways include reading industry reports, following different groups within your genre on social media, and even asking your readers.

6. The Selling Proposition is an understanding of what makes your work unique, even within your genre. Identify what will bring readers and customers to you and bring them back to you. Consider your writing style, your personality, and get feedback from others in this process. You are unique, and you need to let that individuality shine.

7. Cost and Pricing is key. If you have a series written, do you give away or discount the first book to draw people to the rest of the series? Is your market segment small, but active and can stand higher pricing? How many units can you sell at one price over another, and which has the greatest net benefit?

8. Fulfillment and Distribution will detail all of the methods you are using to ship and deliver your product. If you are self-publishing, will you have printed material as well as ebooks? Audiobooks? Amazon/Kindle only?

9. Your Promotion Plan includes the different ways you reach out to your existing customer base, plus future fans and readers. Each of the below items will have varying degrees of research, planning and detail.

a. Your mailing list is a cornerstone. These people tend to be most interested in you, your work and will also be your biggest advocates and first buyers when new work is released. It takes time, but if you treat the fans willing to hand over their email well, they are the ones most likely to help you grow. Also, your mailing list (like your website) is your property, and something which won't disappear because a company changes its rules or goes out of business overnight.

b. Giveaways and promotional pricing.

c. Solicit reviews prior to and post release from your true fans, advance reader teams, on social media, and at in person events.

d. NetGalley is a paid service connecting reviewers with authors. Even if you already have a reader base, NetGalley gets your latest release in front of the reader community.

e. Printed materials like cards, fliers, bookmarks and other SWAG. This material can be used at events, conventions, appearances, or even mailed out as rewards or other promotions.

f. Street teams are groups of fans, often managed through social media, that help promote you out of love for your work. You offer incentives such as being part of your advance reader or beta reader teams, meet ups, and a little more direct personal access.

g. Blog tours connect you with readers by introducing you to readers through popular book, genre, or topical blogs with guest posts.

h. Interviews, whether on live media (TV and radio) written interviews on blogs, newspapers or magazines, or podcasts help connect you with audiences in a personal and direct way.

10. The Launch Plan targets the thirty to sixty days before and after the release of a new book or product. Consider:

a. Online launch parties. Facebook is frequently used for the platform, but Google Hangouts, Twitter, and other social media platforms offer different experiences. While not as effective as they once were, it is still a great way to connect with your true fans.

b. Launch parties at conventions and events, and you can often have a joint launch with others to increase the buzz and decrease related costs.

c. Appearances and readings at bookstores can be arranged by contacting the store manager or working with the promotions departments. Typically chain bookstores will only have authors published through larger houses, but many independent bookstores support and welcome authors independently published, or who are published through smaller publishers.

d. Blog, article, audio and video interviews can be arranged by contacting the program. Most will have submissions guidelines on their website.

e. Targeted giveaways, and rewards for your street team/fans pushing the launch.

11. The Advertising Plan represents much of your investment of capital and expenses as a part of your overall Marketing Plan. Where marketing refers to the overall effort for raising brand and product awareness, advertising is actively communicating to your existing and potential customers in a way to inform and influence their buying decisions. Common methods:

a. Paid online advertising, such as on Facebook, Amazon, Google Ads.

b. Organic advertising through social media by fans sharing out your book, website, promotions, social media presence, and anything else you develop for public consumption. While organic advertising should be a large part of your plan, it is not the cornerstone it has been in prior years as platforms limit commercial material that is not sponsored.

c. Sponsorship in programs at conventions and events.

d. Google ads/Adwords, etc.

e. Attending/sponsoring events and conventions.

f. Other media spots, such as podcasts, website ads, or magazines.

12. Your Conversion Plan should look at how to encourage people to buy your products and services once they have taken the time to visit your website, Facebook page, etc. If you see traffic coming through these sites, but are not seeing an increase in sales, evaluate why your marketing is failing.

In essence, your Marketing Plan pulls together all of the tools you have, and the ways you execute the planning.

Delivering to Your Customers

It may seem a little obvious, but the basis of selling yourself, your brand, and your products is understanding who may be interested. Who is your potential audience?

You are not and cannot be all things to all people. Nor should you be. Most people are passionate about a relatively few things. The better you target your potential audience, the faster you will get a return on your investment of time and resources. The audience interested in language of the fifteenth century will likely have little interest in an industrial convention but may find people i at a historical romance convention. A book on couponing will probably not fare well at a luxury car sales training meeting but may be the hit at the frugal mom meeting.

So how do you find and attract your target audience?

1. Identify and define your target audience:
   a. Who is interested in your product or genre?
   b. Are there specific demographics such as age, gender, education, etc.?
   c. Are there specific personality traits, frustrations or passions for those who want or benefit from your work?
   d. Who can benefit most from your work?
   e. What types of groups or associations would your customer belong to or join?
   f. You may well discover you have multiple ideal target audiences. Your young adult series may appeal both to girls aged 13-17 and soccer moms aged 25-45.
2. Once you have identified your target audiences, build a profile for each. Spend a little time and treat them like a character. What do they like? Dislike? Where do they go out for dinner? What do they watch on television? Is there unique jargon and knowledge for those inside the group?
3. Take the profile you have built (your customer avatar) and do some research. Who shares interest in the key subject matter? Who speaks the technical jargon? What social media and live groups does a person interested in home gardening belong to? What programs talk about and have guests talking about the history of World War II?
4. Who else is in your space? Who are your peers and competitors? Where do they promote their work? Where and when do they speak? On what topics?

5. Who are the biggest influencers in the market? Who hosts the morning show? Who hosts the podcast? Who writes articles about your genre? Once you identify the influencers, you can hone and tweak your message and your presentation.
6. Join groups that interest you. Learn and be a part of their communities. Networking and relationships are two-way streets that can put you on a fast track to your own community.
7. Contribute where your audience goes. Write your own blog and offer to do posts for others. Join social media groups and be active. Be willing to listen. Build your networks and your relationships. Offer your own knowledge. Challenge yourself. If you have become the biggest fish in your pond, then it is time to jump to the lake. Go where you are challenged to learn and grow.
8. Make mistakes. Own them. We have a greater opportunity to learn and grow from failures and mistakes than successes. And if we are honest with ourselves, if everything goes to plan, you are not taking enough risks or stretching yourself enough. To err is human. We all do it, just be honest when it happens, and take responsibility.
9. Be genuine. Be empathetic. Be yourself. Give first. Do not expect a quid pro quo. Earn it.
   The current buzz word (that I have developed a disdain for) is to be authentic. While we speak of developing your persona, those parts you share publicly on social media, in person and at events, still need to be you. Your best you.

Much like the rest of the book, this is a continual and iterative process. Your audience will grow and change. You will as well. You will grow and get better.

So will your audience.

Make Your Pitch

At the heart of every contact with a potential customer is the ability to tell them who you are and what you do. In short, your sales pitch.

Classically, we are used to the idea of making an elevator pitch, and trying to move into a quick close, or if needed, opening the door to the longer sales pitch. The art and science of sales changes quickly not only to follow what is happening in the marketplace, but also often leads the way that we as consumers think. The refinement of the sales pitch is no different. There are a few models that can help you find what works best for you and your product:

- *One Word.* As authors, the one-word pitch is hard. We do like words after all. But sometimes you can refine your subject matter down to the one key word to see if the interest is there to go further. Think about it as the lead in. Heist. Vampires. Romance.
- *Subject Line.* This is the most common idea of a lead into any pitch. How much information do you see packed into effective subject lines on an email? Look at any number of the plethora of newsletters, sales emails (and SPAM) you see come in on a daily basis. What grabs your attention? What sends you immediately to the delete key? Think of this as the pitch used for Facebook ads.
- *Twitter/Elevator Pitch.* The classical elevator pitch has largely been replaced with the "Twitter Pitch." How much can you cram into a few sentences to grab attention, or tell if it does not meet the person's interest?
- *Pixar.* What has become known as the Pixar pitch is learning to tell a concise but complete narrative. It outlines the who, what, and why quickly. "Once upon a time… their average day… then everything changed…. If you are writing non-fiction, or something that provides a material benefit or service, you are including the problem statement and the benefits. For fiction, tell the hook to the story.
- *Question.* We as human beings are wired for resolution. The question pitch triggers our inquisitive nature and need for an answer. What if a grandmother becomes a superhero? What happens if a florist falls into a love triangle between an international banker and an unknown street artist? What does it take to make a living as an author?

You will find that different pitches work better for different medias and audiences. It is a process of trial, error, and refinement. Never miss an opportunity to practice.

Your Presence

Now that you have your brand and persona, it's time to expand your footprint in the world.

There are many ways to build your presence and fan (customer) base, but most fall into one of these categories:
- *Social media:* This is now pervasive in all of our lives, to connect with people is almost a necessity.
- Social media allows you to build and maintain relationships in a way never before possible and have greater reach with minimal investment.

- o The challenge is deciding where to create and maintain your presence, because it does take up one of your most precious resources: Time. Pick the platforms that work for you and your tribe.
- o Remember that anything that happens in cyberspace, stays in cyberspace forever. And goes beyond those boundaries. One unfortunate rant posted in anger, even if deleted, can come back to haunt you months or years later. A picture taken out of context or within certain political climates can have a completely different interpretation at a later date.
- o Many platforms such as Facebook allow you to form open and closed groups. It allows you to create the feeling of exclusivity for your fans and enables them to have a more personal relationship with you and your creative output.
- *Web presence*: Your Internet presence extends well beyond social media; how is largely determined by who you interact with and how you run your business.
- o Your Websites - At a minimum, you should have an author page on the major sites such as Amazon and Goodreads. I'd also suggest having a personal site and if you're so inclined, maintain a blog.
- o Other websites: In addition to the major retail eCommerce sites, you can meet and interact with potential associates, resources and customers via blogs, forums, alternative media outlets, and any number of other social and services sites. Depending on the product you develop as a writer, editor, artist, etc., there are numerous places to meet and discuss any topic from the latest political events, breaking news, sports scores, and even the most niche interests.
- *Traditional Media*: Traditional media presents many opportunities for exposure.
- o Local and national radio, television and print media look for material relevant to current events, and for culturally influential work. If you are a physician writing medical thrillers, you might be consulted about a local outbreak.
- o Events like conventions, meet and greets, festivals, sports and arts are frequently covered by media, and give opportunities to see and meet media personalities.
- *Alternative Media*: Podcasting, blogs, and other websites have exploded in the model of gonzo journalism (think Hunter S. Thompson) and pirate radio.
- *In Person*: This can be the hardest, but also most rewarding form of presence. Doing speaking engagements, conventions and other events allows you to connect in a very personal way with present and future fans, as well as others in your industry.

When building your presence, remember, you're not in this alone. Network and build relationships with others in the business and in your genre. Everyone has a lesson to teach.

As with all businesses, you can only do so much in selling yourself. It's time to bring the rest of the team in to help get your message out there.

The good news, there's a lot of options, and your tribe can help. The bad news, there's a lot of options, and now you're having to depend on others.

You may be asking yourself, what are all these options?

- Marketing and Advertising Services - It may seem a little obvious, but there are services out there to help you get your message out. This can tend to be expensive, and should be part of your budget if you plan to use paid services, including:
  o Publicists and agents
  o Advertising services that build a full strategy
  o Facebook, Goodreads, Google, or other web-based advertising.
  o Targeted traditional media advertising
  o Sponsor events
- Your tribe
  o Fellow authors and publishers can support new products and raise awareness when they come out.
  o Your readers and fans are your best source. They already love and want more of your work, and will help entice new potential fans.
- True fans
  o Your street team - this is your most loyal fan base, and reward them for being so, but ask them to help you grow!
  o These are the people who pre-order every book and travel to an appearance just to tell you hi. They are your lifeblood as an artist, and the difference in success. These are the people you want to cultivate into your street team.
  o They will share every post and re-tweet your musings.
  o Casual fans and random encounters - Social media can raise awareness on a topic or a piece of work faster than ever before. Think about how things "go viral." You can't count on it but cultivate these systems and they can reward you.

These are just a few common examples, but what else do you need to consider when looking at these options?

- Who am I asking to do something for me?
  o When you contract for services, you have a much better potential of having references, reviews about their services and results, and a track record to look at. Be mindful that it is purely a business relationship, and not one of interest or passion.

- In your tribe and among your fan base, requests for support is based on personal relationships, which may be casual or even virtual. When you ask for a favor, craft the message you are asking people to push. Make it as easy as possible. Ask them to share your social media messages, and not for people to do something on their own. Make it as easy as possible.
- What are they expecting, if anything, in return?
  - With paid services (ex. publicists, social media management, ad services), there is the expectation of a contract with specified services in exchange for specific remuneration. It may be running $100 of Google ads, or getting a book tweeted out every time you do the same for someone else in your network. If you've hired an assistant or a publicist, make sure both parties are aware of expectations of what is, and is not expected. It's better to have a potentially uncomfortable conversation up front than to have to clean up the mess later.
  - The reason people share your message can be as simple as they love your work and want you to keep doing it. Appreciate your fans and your tribe. Send out SWAG or do the occasional giveaway for their help. This is a two-way relationship.
- What might they be able to do in my name or with my brand that I don't want, will not serve me, or can even be harmful?
  - The key is to do what you can to control your message. If you are working under a contractual agreement, you have much more control with legal and financial tools to resolve issues.
  - When working with volunteers and fans, you have much less control, so be specific about what you ask them to do. But as we are all aware, memes can take on a life of their own. Use any publicity you can, but closely monitor feedback to adjust for the best results, including anyone using it improperly or acting in a way you don't want to be associated with.

SWAG Away!

Sent With A Gift! Stuff We All Get! No matter what the acronym means to you, we're talking SWAG.

If you've ever been to a trade show, book show, or the fair, you've probably been inundated with everything from bumper stickers to coffee mugs to tote bags. It's stuff you give away to attract attention and reward people for giving you a few minutes of time.

To talk about the basic economics of SWAG, balance the cost and effort of whatever you give away against your potential return. The main point of SWAG is to get attention, and to remind people you exist, not to buy a customer.

Basic level SWAG: This is the material you give out for general advertising, look for low cost, high volumes.

- Business cards - you may not typically think of business cards as SWAG, but they can be if you're creative. Yes, one side has all of your basic info, who you are and what you do. On the other side, if you have something entertaining, people are more likely to keep it, and show it off. For example, if you write dystopian fiction, you could have a card that has checkboxes, and says, "Survive nine apocalypses and your tenth is free!" Or an IT consultant that can creatively name and list the services they provide, "Resurrects dead computers!"

- Bookmarks - Almost every author does bookmarks for themselves and their different works. They start at the most basic, an oversized business card to elaborate ones of high-grade material.

- Postcards for your books or series - These can be different sizes, but like all SWAG, it needs to capture your customer's eye, and be something they want to take with them and not toss on the floor in front of your table. For a particular series, I've done my cards for each book like trading cards.

Mid-tier SWAG: This is usually a little costlier but something to reward your fan base, or most loyal customers. Even if it's not costlier, it can be more unique or help you stand out.

- Stickers - Depending on your customer base, it could be bumper stickers for cars, or smaller ones for phones, laptops, or folders. You want something eye catching, like your logo.

- Temporary tattoos - Again, this could be your logo or something tied to your book. I'd expect this is more targeted for fiction authors but can be a great way to reward and mark your fan base at events.

- Ebooks - Digital short stories or other similar work can be delivered when people sign up for your mailing list, a giveaway on Prolific Works (formerly Insta-freebie), or a bonus download when people buy a book.

- Top tier SWAG: This is the material you don't give away much. In fact, you often can get your fans to buy this SWAG! Or use it as rewards and giveaways T-shirts - a quality t-shirt with your artwork or logo is a walking billboard.

- Squishys - These used to be standard stress balls, but now are available in all sorts of styles and colors. If you write books on technology, maybe you give away ones that look like computers. If you write about magic, they could be little wizards. Children's books could be animals.
- Note pads/post-its - If you provide editing or agency services, something that has your info and logo keeps your name in front of people in a useful way.
- Coffee mugs/water bottles - Beverage containers are great walking billboards not only at events and conventions, but when people take them home.
- Books - If you're an author, giving away a few copies of the first book in a series can bring people to buy the later copies. Electronic formats make this easy and cost effective, and are good incentives for street teams, advance reader copies, or a physical copy as the big prize for people signing up on your mailing list at an event.
- Services - If you're an editor, you can give away a sample edit, or review submission letters.
- Stuff you make - If you're a jeweler as well as a writer, you could give away a piece of your unique work as a reward for a crowdfunding effort, or as a reward for your most supportive people. If you crochet and are a romance writer, you can give away handmade items that are "adult." (Yeah, I've seen that one. Romance writers can be very creative.) A friend of mine sells her crocheted "F-bombs."

Make sure whatever SWAG you use is on brand, and has a targeted use, whether to buy a book, join your mailing list, or provide other value, also make sure it fits your budget, your audience, and represents you!

Your Email List

If you don't have an e-mail list already, finish this section, put this book down, and start working on it. I highly recommend Tammi Labrecque's book, Newsletter Ninja.

If you have a list, are you using it effectively? I know I still am working on it.

What's this list I speak of?

It's one of the best tools to help build and sustain your tribe, and your best customers. It's the list of people to whom you send something on a semi-regular basis. And I'm not just talking about sales pitches. It should be tidbits about what you're doing, upcoming work, appearances, and anything people will find valuable or worth reading.

One thing to note, you want a list of people who are genuinely interested in you and your material. Having a large list does you no good if people do not read your emails, or if they are not your tribe. It can also cost you money, as most email list services charge you based on your number of emails and subscribers. No, not 100% of people will read every email, but you want your list to be your tribe, and your customers.

The most important fact about your list? It's yours. Just like your website, but better. If a social media platform changes its rules or goes away tomorrow? It doesn't affect your list. But you get to know how to reach your readers and connect with them.

How do I build a list as an author, editor, or publisher? Or any sort of artist?

There are a lot of schools of thought and many resources available on the topic of list building. What works for one person, genre, or product may not work for others. My basic rule is this; any time I get an opportunity to grow my list, I do it.

- Offer a gift or incentive for people to sign up, be it a free story, other product or service, or a discount.
- Viral giveaway contests help you get new subscribers, but make sure your incentive is attractive to your target customer. Giving away an iPad may bring you people signing up, but not necessarily your audience.
- Rewards for people who share your information helps build your tribe. This is especially true of your street team. Incentivizing people to share keeps advertising costs down, and is more likely to attract people in your target audience.
- Webinars or online event - I'll offer specials to anyone who has already or does sign up for my list by a certain date, and live events like this online let a larger number of people get to know you and your products.
- At events and personal appearances, I have an app on a electronic tablet (or will use a sign-up sheet) and will often will give away premium SWAG to one lucky person that signs up.

- I have a widget for people to sign up on my website. A pop-up window can be very successful, but don't hammer people with it. Have it solicit people after they have spent time on your site, and don't have it solicit every time. There are many plugins for Wordpress that can handle this.
- I include links in my ebooks and instructions in the print copies to ask people to sign up. I include it in my biographies, any time I do a guest blog, and every time I do any kind of appearance.

Note: Do not buy an e-mail list from someone else or a service. There is a term for sending people emails that haven't signed up and asked for it. SPAM, and not the kind in a can. This will both irritate someone who might have been a potential reader and can be illegal.

Instead, build relationships with others in the field and genre. Swap guest posts in each other's newsletters and invite people to follow you that way.

I can sense your next question. How do I maintain my list, and send content to it?

Beyond manually maintaining the list in your mail client, and sending out e-mails (and if you use this approach, most will be flagged as SPAM and not delivered), there are services and options. A few common services are:

- MailChimp - **http://mailchimp.com/** - The service is free up to a certain number of subscribers and is fairly robust in features. Paid accounts are more powerful.
- Mailerlite - **https://www.mailerlite.com/** - A simple yet powerful email automation service, popular with authors.
- Feedblitz - **https://www.feedblitz.com**/ - powerful, yet cost effective for small and medium sized companies, and is popular with bloggers.
- Constant Contact - **https://www.constantcontact.com**/ - A powerful, but expensive engine. It goes well beyond email lists and is good for medium to larger sized businesses.
- Mad Mimi - **https://madmimi.com** - Strong on newsletter functionality and has some large corporate clients.
- Campayn - **http://campayn.com/** - Simple to use, and well-suited for smaller and medium sized operations.
- Campaign Monitor - **https://www.campaignmonitor.com** - Another robust tool with a large client base.

I'm not recommending any particular engine as each has its strengths and weaknesses based on the market you serve and your budget. In addition to these, dozens of excellent campaign automation engines that will help you manage and grow your e-mail list, generate professional, attractive newsletters and messages for your fan base. Most solutions offer a free version or a trial period. Try out several to find what best meets your needs and your style. Most require very little technical skill to use, and most will have plugins to work with most major website engines, especially Wordpress.

Some design considerations for your sign-up form:

- Keep it simple.
- Collect only the info you need, and that people will be happy to share. All you really need is the e-mail address.

There are legal requirements and considerations to maintaining an email list:

- You must provide a title for the e-mail that is informative and not misleading about your content.
- You must provide a way for people to opt out from receiving further messages and obey those requests.
- You must provide a physical mailing address to allow for complaints and other correspondence.
- Be explicit about your privacy policy, and that you aren't selling your list. Anything you include in your privacy and use notices is legally binding.
- All of these, and other requirements are now part of the General Data Protection Regulation (GDPR) which went into effect in May of 2018. These regulations apply to all citizens of the European Union and to anyone acting, residing, or doing business inside the EU, even if they are not citizens or residents of the EU.

The good news, any of the above services can and do keep you compliant on the last two requirements. The title and your message are up to you.

Once you select a tool and have some followers, what can your list do for you? Once you're on the way to having a list, what now?

Content is always the tricky part. You need to provide content your followers will enjoy and benefit from without being spammy.

I suggest doing a newsletter. The type and frequency will depend on your subject matter. If you write about any type of current events, it's easy to do something daily or weekly. You treat it like a newspaper for your readers. If you write self-help, it could be a daily affirmation. For fiction it's a question of what you have for your readers.

Street Teams

When I was in college in the late 1980's, we had a strong music scene in Columbia, SC. In addition to fun local acts like Hootie and the Blowfish, we weren't far from Athens, GA, and pulled in a lot of national acts. You found out who was playing at the different clubs by someone handing out flyers, or even the bands themselves. While usually not that organized, bigger acts and promoters might even be pushing SWAG or free tickets to get a crowd.

This is what would come to be known as a street team.

As an author, you can adopt the same strategy. Not necessarily your fans standing on street corners handing out bookmarks and asking them to join your fandom. In the digital age, think about them as your true fans, the evangelists who can and love to support their favorite authors.

- Members of your street team can:
- Be members of your ARC (advance reader copy) team and leave reviews soon after a book launches.
- Attend (bolster numbers) when you have an in person or virtual launch party.
- Pass out SWAG at conventions.
- Post and share on social media.
- Suggest your books for their book clubs.
- What goes into building a street team?
- It's worth remembering that these are volunteers. They may even be people you've never met beyond social media and are scattered all over the country or globe. They are valuable, but you are also entrusting part of your brand to them. Some vetting is required.
- Have a Facebook group for your fans. Those who are most active and supportive are great candidates.
- See who shows up at all of your signings and conventions.
- See who trusted members of your street team recommend.
- Have an application process. Google Forms works well for this.
- Once you start identifying candidates, have a few more questions meant to make sure they are not only a good fit for you and your street team, but that your team model is a good fit for them as well.
- Ask if they are part of any other street teams. Active readers often are.
- Ask what of your work they have read, and what they do and don't like about it.
- Ask how they would like to see your book promoted. What would speak to them.
- Who else are they reading?

- And last, take care of your street team once it's built. People will come and go over time, but value and respect them.
- Host an exclusive Facebook or Google Hangout group so they get some exclusive access to you and treat them like part of the team.
- Have SWAG for them. Have kits to welcome them, be it a digital email kit with your rules, and info on how to promote you, and even SWAG for them to hand out if appropriate.
- Have giveaways and rewards for your street team. Be careful so it's not seen as compensation for leaving reviews. It can be books, SWAG, even meet and greets at events.

It takes time and experimentation to build a street team but worth it in every way.

Speaking Engagements

In your career in the publishing industry, at some point you are likely to come face-to-face with your adoring public, and hopefully attract new fans in the process. For many non-fiction and professional/technical presenters, becoming a writer and speaker is a natural progression of their career.

Public speaking and presentations take many forms. Each has its benefits and challenges. Public speaking is often reported as people's number one fear, beating out unemployment, clowns, and death. Yes, there are people that would prefer to die than speak in front of a few people. Fortunately for me, I am not one of those people, but it takes time to become comfortable.

If you are unaccustomed to or uncomfortable with public speaking, or just want to improve your style and delivery, organizations such as Toastmasters International (https://www.toastmasters.org) is an excellent group and resource provide a safe place for practice and critique.

I mentioned this chapter to a friend in a writing group I belong to, and after shuddering, they asked "Why would any writer want to stand up and speak. I write to avoid people." I am not shoving any of you in front of a crowd and it's not for everyone, but here are some ways you can use speaking to advance your brand and business:

- If you operate in any business of consulting or coaching, or are a subject matter expert, speaking is one of the best ways to advertise and sell your services. Speaking becomes key in all of your business activities and helps develop your reputation in your field. Once you have built a name, individual and keynote speeches allow you to highlight yourself and your expertise. These can be done for small, targeted groups or large audiences. They can range from a few minutes to hours of lecture. After any given talk, there are always some people who will want your books, with autographs of course. Plus, any videos, courses, or other products you may have.

- Participating on panels at events has many of the benefits of being a solo speaker with the added advantage of having others to converse with in a more relaxed form of presentation. Being on a panel with others also lends some credibility from the others you share the panel with, and helps you network in your community.

- Hosting a podcast or video cast puts you in control of the program and the message you are interested in delivering. If you have guests as a part of your show, you are building your network. Both you and your guest get to take advantage of the advertising and media. And it is a way to build a following.

- Appearing on and being interviewed for a podcast, videocast, radio or television show is an easy way without physically being in front of large audiences.

Now that I've talked you into standing up and facing your adoring throngs, you need to go out and line them up. How do you do this, you ask?

Look for the groups and programs focused on your interests and expertise. If you are a counselor and coach for adoptions, look for the support groups and programs. If you are a technology manager, the Project Management Institute and other groups host meetings and conferences. Romance writer? Romance conventions. If there is an interest, there are programs. If there is a program, they need guests and content. Network, and apply, send out press releases, and make some phone calls.

You will find the more programs you do, the easier it is to get additional engagements. And this is one of the big functions of a publicist is to use their connections to pave these roads for you.

Sales Channels

"Our greatest weakness lies in giving up. The most certain way to succeed is always to try just one more time."
-Thomas Edison

You've done all the hard work. Your product and/or service is ready. You have prepared to introduce it to your adoring fans, and the people yet to become your adoring fans.

What's left?

Making your product available so they can actually buy it. Welcome to the wide world of Sales Channels.

Sales Channels can be categorized in one of two ways:

- *Direct Sales Channels* are where you as the producer are in front of your customers. In short, load up your car with books and head off to an event.
- *Indirect Sales Channels* involve a middle-man between you and your customer. You dropped your product off and the local bookstore has stocked it on the shelves.

If you are purely traditionally published, some of this will be handled without your involvement. If your work is self-published, you are responsible for all of it.

This section explores the common sales channels for authors, and how to use them rot reach customers and develop true fans.

In-person Events (Hand-to-Hand Sales)

For most people, the majority of direct sales will come from in-person events. This may be as simple as having a booth at an art show or convention, or as complex as being part of a live event where you are either the host or participant.

The biggest benefit of direct sales is a personal connection your customer. It gives you an opportunity to turn them into a "true fan."

The down side is that these tend to be time consuming, and there are no guarantees that you can or will connect with your customers.

I personally enjoy doing conventions and do a lot of different events throughout the year, with a lot of different purposes. Even working at a volunteer or charity event, I always have a few cards and bookmarks on me and almost always have a few books in the trunk or with me.

I'm not one for the hard sell, at least for my work. Instead, I look to engage with potential customers and readers, and depending on what the event is, I change my tone and approach. The one consistent thing for me is my willingness to talk to people and tell them I'm a consultant and an author. If the conversation goes that way, and if people are interested, I'll give them a card, and sometimes even pull a book out to show them. I've even paid more than a few bar tabs that way.

Quite frequently, I meet other writers or people who want to be writers. In those conversations, I am free with advice, but also can be very direct about the good and bad. If someone is not interested in what I write, I'm also happy to share other authors who might interest the person.

Admittedly, I am more extroverted than many people (and most writers) and have learned to enjoy engaging with people. It's not easy for everyone, but the art of connecting with people is a key to building your brand and your market.

Your Website

Your Website can be either or both a direct and indirect channel for sales at the same time.

As a direct channel, you can sell copies through your website, often giving a premium such as autographs or other SWAG to entice people to buy from you directly.

As an indirect channel, your website should have a page for each book or series and include links to buy the books through a retailer.

The design of your website should not only focus on engaging people with your brand and the value of your work but also facilitate buying it easily.

In total, your website is the real estate you own to educate, entertain, engage and influence readers, and lead them to a buying decision. Every section should be relevant to you and your readers, and have clear "calls to action" to enable people to sign up for your mailing list or buy books. (For more information on designing your website, refer to the Tools of the Trade section.)

Virtual Events

Virtual events such as a Facebook party sales launch or Google Hangouts are indirect channels, even though you are directly engaging with potential readers. While not as effective as they once were, they are still a good way to set time aside to engage with your most avid readers and bring in a few new ones.

As an example, a Facebook launch party is typically structured this way:

- The host (and author with the new launch) invites other authors to co-host the event.
- The event can be run as an all-day event, for a few hours over one or several evenings depending on how many people are involved and how much the host wants to do.
- The host gives each guest author one or more slots to do a Q&A, a reading (Facebook Live is good for this) or other fun activity. The guest authors should also promote the event and their time to bring over some of their readers to grow the audience. Commonly, these are half hour slots. The host introduces the guest, and thanks them at the end of their time.
- Engagement should be both directed to help all the authors grow their social media followings and mailing lists, as well as sell books.
- Incentivize your readers to engage with giveaways for joining your mailing list or social media fan base, or even just for joining the party.
- Facebook lunch parties are also a good forum in which to solicit reviews and invite new members to join your ARC (advance readers) team.
- It should NOT be a hard sell... sell... sell... event but geared toward engagement. In most cases, the virtual event will drive sales to retailers rather than direct sales.

In short, focus on this is as a chance to engage with, and thank your current and future readers in advance!

Large Retail Chains

Retail chain bookstores and general retailers carrying books have been in decline for the last decade. The growth of ebooks, Amazon's capture of the market, and the general contraction in the retail market have all contributed. This being said, Amazon has launched their first brick and mortar locations.

Large retailers, whether primarily a bookstore or general retailer, typically only stock inventory from the largest houses for traditionally published authors. They carry most inventory on consignment, meaning only the largest publishers can carry the cost and risk. Unsold copies are returned, or the covers returned for credit and the books destroyed. Having titles in a retailer does not count towards copies sold.

Shelf space is often negotiated with publishers and is valuable real estate for the retailer. In addition to the cost of consigning the books, end caps and premium shelf space comes at an additional cost.

Many retailers will host you as an author for the books carried in their location and allow you to have a signing.

Depending on the channels you use for self-published work, many retailers can option to order your book for a customer upon request. Topical local and regional books (i.e. the haunted history of New Orleans) may also be carried by larger chains from small and independent publishers.

Independent Bookstores

For the small publisher, hybrid and self-published author, independent bookstores can be excellent outlets to get your work on the shelves. The American Booksellers Association (http://bookweb.org) sponsors a newsletter featuring indie titles, but can also connect you with independent bookstores around the country. Many states and regions also have their own associations for independent booksellers. You will find similar associations in other countries.

- Independents typically are receptive to smaller publishers and self-published work, but will have criteria the author/publisher needs to meet for consideration.
- Titles on the shelves are often on consignment, and not bought by the retailer. This means you as the author carry the cost of providing inventory, and are not paid unless the titles sell. They also are subject to being returned to the author.
- Understand the conditions by which the retailer can and will carry titles. Review the consignment contract, understand any additional costs (like shelf space charges), how long a title may sit on a shelf (often 90 day cycles), how much you will make per sold copy.
- With independents who elect to carry your work, you are responsible for delivery and management of product on the shelves.
- Independents frequently host events such as readings and signings.

Online and Ebooks

Online book sales passed traditional bookstores as the top delivery channel in 2014. The margin continues to widen, but the pace has slowed. While most retailers and many publishers have their own online bookstores, Amazon is by far the single largest online retailer.

As of 2017, 17% of traditionally published books were sold as ebooks through one of multiple platforms, and 77% still in print format. 5.6% were in audio.

Conversely, the vast majority of self-published books sold are ebooks, with only an estimated 3% are sold in print format. For online book sales, ebooks often carry a higher royalty as a percentage of sales and the author can net as much from an ebook sale as a more expensive title in print.

Ebook platforms like Kindle and Nook, or apps on tablet and smartphone platforms supported rapid growth of the ebook market in a way not previously possible. ECommerce distributors such as Amazon, Barnes and Noble and Lulu.com provide Print on Demand services, and coupled with ebook offerings gives the small press and independent author the same capabilities as the largest publishing houses.

We are also seeing a change in the book market where ebook lending libraries and subscription services are emerging to give people access to books in the same way Netflix did for movies. This delivery channel will continue morph and emerge as a marketplace (think KDP select). Consumers have created the demand for on-demand content at fixed prices. It also gives consumers the option to read a few pages and feel less pressure to finish a book than if they'd bought it at retail. For authors, this is a mixed bag. It gives you the opportunity to reach new readers, but the payout amounts have greater variability.

As of 2018, the overall ebook market seems. To have leveled out, and print media has picked up some growth. I expect we will continue to see growth in the ebook markets, and it will allow for innovation in content length, style, and offer multimedia options print cannot. With the expansion of augmented and virtual reality, reading a book is becoming an even greater immersive experience.

Interviews

Hosting or being interviewed on television, radio, videocast, podcast, article, blog, etc. can bring an author or service provider a great deal of exposure. The appearance and advertising on the programs provide the author a chance to build and expand their brand and connect with fans in a more personal way. The core benefit of interviews is sharing yourself to connect with someone else's audience.

As a sales channel, often this will lead to indirect sales by driving traffic to particular retailers.

Libraries

Libraries can be an excellent distribution channel. While you will only sell a relatively small number of copies for a potentially large number of readers, it can provide both credibility to the quality of the work and give availability to people who may not otherwise get it.

Amazon and Kindle

"Some of the most innocuous inventions have proven earth-shattering. With reverberations felt around the planet. The internet is the poster child for disruptive technology, but even such inventions as Amazon's Kindle and Apple's iPod have rocked their respective industries by changing how we entertain ourselves." - Lynda Resnick

Since Kindle (via Amazon) is the largest channel (800-pound silverback gorilla) for ebooks in the market, and also offers the most options and innovations for publishers, authors, and readers, it deserves its own chapter.

Kindle was not the first ebook reader platform, but it led the digital book revolution. I was hesitant at first to get a Kindle; I had tried a prior incarnation of ebook reader. At the time, I traveled 48 weeks a year for work, plus some more for personal trips. I spent more than my fair share of time in airports and hotels, and it was common for me to read 3-4 books per week, plus research materials or keeping current professionally. This leads to a lot of paper weight.

I was given a first-generation Kindle as a gift, and quickly adapted to the technology. I have thousands of ebooks in my library at this point, but even so, I love physical books. To this day, there are books I have in both mediums, and I am far from unique.

Amazon's next big change was to roll out Kindle Unlimited (KU) in July 2014, a subscription service that allowed readers unlimited access to books for just $10 a month. The reception by readers was mostly positive, finally a Netflix for books! The reaction from authors and publishers was and still is mixed.

Kindle Unlimited was doing to independent authors what Spotify did to musicians. By offering books to subscribers essentially for free, they were potentially lowering the revenue that an author or publisher could make from each book. And despite Amazon's best efforts, there is a subculture of authors who continuously work to game the system.

In this article we explore how Kindle and KU has evolved and its current impact on authors with a thought towards what may be forthcoming.

Kindle Unlimited & KDP Select: A History

The KDP Select Global Fund is a pot of money that goes to authors whose books are downloaded through Amazon's ebook programs. Authors who enrolled their ebooks in KDP (Kindle Direct Publishing) Select prior to the launch of KU could have their books downloaded for free by Kindle owners who were allotted one free ebook per month through the Kindle Owners Lending Library. In the days prior to KU, the Global Fund totaled around one-million dollars and was divided proportionally amongst the authors whose books were downloaded.

In July 2014 with the introduction of KU, the Global Fund increased to $2.4 M, and grew over the next year as more readers signed up for KU. The Global Fund increased to $11.5 M by July 2015. Today it sits just shy of $23 M (as of July 2018) and grows steadily every month.

For the first year of KU, payouts were simple: Each author was paid every time someone downloaded and read at least 10% of their book. When KU was a year old, in June 2015, Amazon announced they would begin paying participating authors by pages read, instead of by number of books downloaded. At the same time, they introduced KENPC (Kindle Edition Normalized Page Count), which accounted for type size and line spacing to prevent anyone from cheating the system and artificially making their books longer. Amazon calculated the payout per page by beginning with their monthly KDP Select Global Fund and dividing it by the total number of (KENP) pages read. That first month it was decreed that each page was worth $0.005779.

As more readers and more authors entered into the KU system, the Global Fund size did not compensate for the increasing number of pages read every month, so the payout per page read dropped steadily in 2015.

In January of 2016, Amazon announced yet another change in how they would pay authors with the introduction of KENPC v2.0 (Kindle Edition Normalized Page Count). This was supposed to standardize for additional spacing and text features. Some authors saw their page counts, and thus their total potential payout per book, drop, while others saw them rise. Amazon claimed that the average change across all KDP titles would be under 5%, but individual authors saw up to 10% changes in page length.

An additional change implemented in V2.0 was the capping of payouts at page 3,000 for longer titles. This affected mostly dictionaries and large reference books but did have some implications for larger boxed sets as well. Since these changes, the payout per page has increased back up toward $0.005 per page.

At the time of this writing (the summer of 2018), the rules continue to change frequently. Many of the changes are because of small numbers of authors who game the system in different ways, leading Amazon to implement new algorithms and requirements. Examples include putting tables of contents in the front of your book instead of the back or omitting links in the front to carry the reader to the last page to connect to social media or the author's website (see more in Kindle Controversies). A recent tactic that is being clamped down on, is for an author to release a collection, where only the last story is new, prompting the reader to jump to the end of the book.

These rules only apply to books in the KDP select library. Violations are increasingly leading to authors accounts being dropped and banned, often catching other authors as collateral damage in the process.

Authors do have a choice of whether or not their book is included in KU. An author can simply opt out of KU altogether by not enrolling their book in KDP Select. This decision proves agonizing for many authors, and there are authors who make good arguments for both sides.

Hugh Howey, a successful indie author who credits Amazon with much of his success, said in an interview with Digital Book World, "Kindle Unlimited is just one example of the enormous sums of money an author misses out on by going with a major publisher. We're talking $150,000,000 a year going directly to authors, and if you sign with a major publisher, you are taking yourself out of that pool."

However, some authors argue that inclusion in KDP Select (and by extension, KU) authors are losing out on other revenue streams and becoming increasingly more reliant on Amazon.

Kindle Controversies

Kindle Unlimited has sparked its fair share of complaints and controversies.

From a payment perspective, the biggest downside to KU from the beginning has been that authors no longer get paid for books that readers borrow and never read. We all have that stack of books we keep telling ourselves we want to read, but never seem to get to.

In the early days of indie ebook authorship, if your cover and blurb were good enough to prompt a sale, you got paid. Now the game has changed and rewards increasingly higher quality, engaging content. As competition increases, covers and blurbs become more important in making ebooks stand out from the crowd, but the crux of success depends on the content of a book and quality of storytelling.

The most notable and recent controversy concerned the placement of the table of contents in books enrolled in KU. Some authors were placing a link at the beginning of their ebooks which directed the reader to a table of contents that lived at the back of the book. Since the number of pages read by a reader (which is what the payout is based off of) is measured by noting the furthest page in a book that a reader views, some believed that authors were cheating the system by preemptively pushing readers to the end of their books. It turns out that this was not as impactful as many believed, though a few people managed to make a lot of money out of the tactic.

I dive deeper into this example because it represents the good and bad of KU. Formatting decisions that make sense for the reader can be gamed to the benefit of a few bad actors. It means a greater gap between the ebook formatting and print copies, and can even mean having two different ebook formats between the one in KU, and the one for sale.

This policy changes also meant a lot of authors had their work pulled from the shelves until they could meet the new formatting requirements.

Amazon reviews are a common issue among authors. It's hard enough to get them from readers, but we often see some or all of them being stripped from a title without notification or reason. While Amazon does not publish their algorithms, there is evidence that having connections on social media can be enough for reviews to be removed, on the basis they are not impartial. This becomes a conflict where we as authors and business people are encouraged to build connections via social media and our networks, to also have those connections used against us. I argue it is better to have the connection with the true fans than the review, but this is another example where Amazon can be draconian in their decisions.

From a business perspective, most of the decisions we see from Amazon seem to be made with the customer's best interests. Amazon's customers. While at times implications of these policies feel like they target you, it's a decision made to punish the few gaming the system, but it does affect us all.

How Do Authors Drive KU Borrows?

The same marketing tactics that work for selling books also work for driving KU borrows:

- Promote your title to readers (through your email list, Facebook or Google ads, features on deal sites)
- Drive enough sales or download volume to rise in the bestseller charts
- Activity on the title spurs Amazon's algorithm to recommend your book to other readers with similar tastes
- Follow up sales continue after your promotion has run; KU borrows turn into KENP read
- Run another promotion ninety-days later once momentum declines

KU has two fundamental perks for indie authors actively marketing their titles:

1. It is thought that Amazon gives preferential treatment to KU titles, although there is no definitive proof. A glance through the Kindle Top Charts shows a large portion of the best performing books are eligible for KU. Perhaps this is simply because a KU borrow counts the same as a normal sale or download, so it is easier for these titles to climb the charts. The effect of this is discussed in the most recent author earnings report.
2. Major publishing houses have limited availability of their titles through the KU program. Competition within the KU program (which includes the books listed in the Kindle Countdown Deal charts, and elsewhere) are other indies or small presses. This reduces the competition with the large presses and best-known titles.

The primary difference when marketing a title enrolled in KU is how quickly you can measure the results of your efforts. For a title not enrolled in KU measurement is simple: authors watch their sales graph spike, and then watched halo sales (post advertising follow-up sales) come through in the following days. Authors tally up the total earnings from the promotion and compare it to the time and money spent actively marketing the title.

The standard formula

RETURN = Total Sales – Amazon Royalty – Marketing Cost

For a title that is enrolled in KU, there is an additional component to measure: KENP read.

The challenge here is twofold:

1. Readers who borrow a title during the promotion may not read that book until 6 months later. There is an extensive time lag between the promotion and the results of the promotion

2. Authors don't know what the payout per page will be until the following month. So it is difficult to ascribe a value to pages read that do come through in the days following the promotion.

The KU formula:
RETURN = (Total Sales − Amazon Royalty) + (KENP pages read * KENP payout rate) − Marketing Cost

Many authors make a best guess by using the prior month's payout per page to get to an approximate value of the KENP read in the weeks following a promotion. Sophisticated authors will look back at promotions over a three- or six-month window to aggregate the full effect, and corresponding full cost of their promotional activity, to account for the lag.

What's Next for Amazon KDP Select and Kindle Unlimited?

Kindle Unlimited has changed the way many people read books. By giving independent authors an arena in which they can sell their books without competition from mainstream publishers, KU has empowered them to find audiences in new ways. But all the while, Amazon reminds authors that they hold the keys to the coffers and can change the rules. (It's impossible to predict what new perks and programs Amazon will release in the coming years but being at the top of the ebook and book markets appears to be a top priority.) KU is a boon for voracious readers, and a great place to introduce yourself and hook them, even if only a few of your titles are in the pool.

Authors still do have control over many things: whether to enroll in KDP Select at all, the packaging of each book and the quality of the content inside. Successful authors focus on these elements and experiment with programs like KDP Select to determine the best path to success for each of their titles.

If you decide to self-publish some or all of your work, I cannot give a good recommendation as to what is the better option, to either go exclusively with Amazon and the benefits it brings, or to "go wide" and sell through the myriad of other platforms including Barnes & Noble's Nook, Kobo, iBooks, and so on. I know authors who have been successful at both strategies, and many I know change their approach depending on what the market is doing at the time.

Going Deep vs. Going Wide

For self-published authors, there is a continuous debate about exclusivity with Amazon. Frequently this is referred to as going deep (exclusive to Amazon) or going wide (using other distributors).

The short answer is, it's your choice. I know authors doing well under both models. If you go exclusive under Amazon, your ebooks can earn up to 70% royalties and enter Kindle Unlimited. By going wide, you are able to reach an audience that may not use Amazon or Kindle. A large percentage of authors are exclusive to Amazon, so if you go wide, this also means you are often competing against fewer books and authors on distributors like Nook, iBooks, and Kobo.

Also note, you can make this choice on a book-by-book basis. You may have some titles go wide, and others deep to maximize exposure and revenues by title. You also have an option to take a book out of exclusivity from Amazon. Each KDP Select period is ninety days, and if you elect to take a book wide, you can drop from the program after that period.

One strategy I have seen authors take is to enlist a book in KDP Select during the launch period when they have the most sales, and then go wide three or six months later.

You are responsible for choosing what works best based on your goals, and what is happening in the market at that time.

No matter what path you choose, make sure the actions you take are ethical, benefit a long career, and not targeting the short-term money. Being an author is a long-tail game, and you need to plan in those terms.

The Launch

I would say, as an entrepreneur everything you do - every action you take in product development, in marketing, every conversation you have, everything you do - is an experiment. If you can conceptualize your work not as building features, not as launching campaigns, but as running experiments, you can get radically more done with less effort.
- Eric Ries

Product launch strategies are a blend of art and science which determines how successful any book will be. Even while you are still writing your first work, you should be cultivating an audience through social media and your website, plus using other mediums (writing websites, flash fiction contests, podcasts) to showcase your brand and your style.

Of course, if you have an established audience, a launch becomes easier because there are people who know you exist. But a large audience comes with its own challenges.

For novels and longer work, the launch process can start as soon as you start writing the book. Novellas and book series run in a continuous marketing cycle. Looking at a sample long term launch process, here is what it looks like from a high level:

- Build interest and engage fans over time. This is an ongoing process, and never really starts or ends. You work in tidbits you learn from research, little views of your writing process, and give the occasional progress update. Let fans comment, you never know when a good idea can come up.
- Ninety days before the book release, send queries out to podcasts and blog tours to line up interviews.
- When you are closing in on your release date, do a cover reveal. It could be 10 - 60 days from release, or less, depending on when you get the artwork.
- Run paid ads and increase organic social engagement to drive people on social media and sign up on your mailing list and check out the new release.
- Thirty days out, engage your advance readers, get them copies, and prepare them to leave reviews in the first few days after release.
- Two to four weeks before release, start doing the podcasts and guest blog spots you scheduled. These should run for up to a month after the release.
- If you or your publisher line up pre-sales, let your circle know.
- Start paid advertising when the book is released pointing to your distributors.

- Send out your newsletter to your followers with the new release. You should have been teasing the release in the weeks and months leading up to the book, depending on how frequently you do newsletter, and have new published releases.
- Facebook launch parties are no longer that effective but can still be a way to engage with your true fans, and ARC team.
- After the book is released, continue engagement and advertising for thirty to ninety days or more. and paid advertising can run long, but is often ineffective after a period.

Note: These time frames may vary depending on the specifics of your market, agenda, and goals. It is common for paid ads to be run for long cycles.

Be Your Brand

"A great brand is a story that's never completely told. A brand is a metaphorical story that connects with something very deep — a fundamental appreciation of mythology. Stories create the emotional context people need to locate themselves in a larger experience."
— Scott Bedbury

No matter the size of your business, one of the keys is branding. There are very few places on the planet where the Coke logo is unknown. If I showed you the Nike swoosh, you'd instantly think, "Just Do It."

In creative enterprises, the artist is the brand. This means, you are your own brand. Your brand will have the personality and the life you give it.

So own it.

But what is a brand? Is it a logo? A slogan? A jingle?

All of these identify a brand, but by definition, your brand is the way of communicating who you are, what you do, where you can be found, when you are delivering, why you do what you do and how it benefits your customers.

Most of all, your personal brand is your reputation. It's not any one book or interview or your social media presence. It is how people know you, and what you're known for, so make sure your reputation is based on the best version of who you really are.

What are the factors you need to consider when building your brand?

- Are you going to operate under your given name, or a nom-de-plume?
- What persona do you want to build into your brand?
- How do you want to be seen and known in public?
- Do you need a logo to go with the name?
- Do you have a tagline that identifies you?
- What is the voice of your brand?
- What are you willing to do to build and protect your brand?
- What is your story?

Let's look at each of these in depth:

Why should you consider using a pen name?

I would argue the use of a pen name depends on what writing and services you provide. If you speak publicly on professional topics, your name, your resume and your experience are your brand. The same goes if you're telling your personal story. It's why people engage you.

But what if you write fiction? Write in multiple genres? Provide other services?

For example, if you write certain types of fiction, a pen name can provide a lot of benefit. For example, if you write tyrannosaurus rex boardroom erotica (congratulations Chuck Tingle on your Hugo nomination), you may want a degree of separation from the rest of your personal and professional life. It also allows you to build a social media world completely separate from friends and family, protecting them from your fame. (An unfortunate fact of being a public figure is sometimes you get unwanted attention.)

Also consider, if you write science fiction, historical drama, and have a political column, you might consider a separate name for each line and genre. Even if you are public that all of those names are yours, fans know what to expect when they look for titles under a given name. Conversely, some readers will dismiss reading work by someone if they write in other genres; such as a research scientist who also writes science fiction, or a horror author who also writes romance. These apparent conflicts can be a professional and branding disaster.

Who is the public you?

Having a public persona to go with your art and your business can help you manage the public side of your life. If you do public events including signings, conventions or media, putting on your persona can equip people the shy and introverted to be more outgoing, or those who are more brash to put on the figure they want their public to see. You might even consider having a specific wardrobe for each persona, making it easier to prepare your public self.

Keep in mind, any time you are in public, wear that persona like armor, and protect it like it's made of tissue paper. Your persona and the way your fans perceive you are the cornerstones of your brand.

How do you want to be seen in public?

Whether you adopt a persona or not, be aware and conscious of your public self. Consider it even when you're posting cat videos online. Ask yourself, is this what your followers want to see?

I'm not suggesting that you not be yourself. I'm suggesting you make it the best version of yourself, your true self, and share that with the public. Project the person you want to be, and the one you want to share with the world.

Should I have a logo?

To me, this is a personal choice, but in modern culture, we associate pictures and logos with brands more quickly than anything else. If you have a small image people will easily associate with you any time they see it, you get a lot more options for SWAG and advertising. And it's an easier way of keeping your work in the minds of your fans, and make them feel like they are in an exclusive club.

As with all artwork, consider how it looks in all respects. If you want cautionary tales, look into memes about letter spacing on signs.

What's my line?

A tagline is that short slogan or catchphrase identifying you and your product. Apple's "Think Different" campaign and slogan is one all creative people can live by. If you're a speaker or entertainer, your tagline could be the phrase everyone knows you by. In writing, it could be that key idea or concept you look to communicate with all of your work.

What's the voice of your brand?

Just like in writing, your brand should have its own voice. This means it has a consistent tone and message. For example, compare the websites of James Patterson (http://www.jamespatterson.com), J. K Rowling (https://www.jkrowling.com), Stephen King (https://stephenking.com) and John Scalzi (https://whatever.scalzi.com). Each has the basic framework of a bio for the author, their work and how to buy it, as well as a media kit. At the same time, they each have a significantly different look and feel reflecting their genres and their public persona. They share different levels of their personal and professional lives. The visual representation and the language used all come together to represent the author and their brand.

What are you willing to do to build and protect your brand?

This question is often the most important one you'll ask yourself. What are you willing to do to build and protect your business, your products and your name, and what are you not willing to do?

The idea is open ended, but you should consider what you may need to do from a personal, professional, business and legal viewpoint. How many hours do you need to work to achieve your goals? Are you willing to travel and do promotions? Can you be disciplined to produce work and meet deadlines? Are you ready to face inevitable criticism and reviews?

What's your story?

Pulling all of these parts together will tell your story as a creator, a brand, and as a product. Every story has a narrative, and your brand should feature you as its hero. Are you the hero of your own story, or the sidekick?

Nothing Ever Goes Away

In the age of the internet and social media, anything can happen and the world is informed at the speed of light.

Bad news travels fast, and on the internet, not only does it spread, it never forgets.

Too many people have learned the hard way that there is no real such thing as privacy on the internet. Even the most private images and messages can be shared. A comment made in passing can come back to haunt you a decade later (at the time of this writing, James Gunn is getting the boot from Disney for an old tweet, for which he has long since apologized).

As an author and creator, passions drive us. It is easy to post something on social media, send an e-mail, or a text in the heat of the moment. There are no guarantees how it will be understood by the receiving audience.

Some messages are not meant to be shared.

As you build and protect your brand, you must consider everything you do and post. Any message can go viral. Sharing divisive opinions can solidify an audience and alienate others.

Yes, sometimes we are called to make a stand, even knowing that it can have negative consequences. Make those decisions consciously and with intent.

Consider how a joke, the picture of a cosplay, or rash statement can be taken out of context.

And most of all, know that even if it's "deleted" or "private," it's out there. Somewhere. Just waiting for you to be famous.

Selling Yourself

At the core of every business is the need to sell the products and services being offered. As a general rule, you either love to sell, or hate it. For many of us, "sales" is even a dirty word, carrying the connotations of manipulation.

Now consider, as a creative type, you're not only selling some random product, you are selling your creative output. You are selling a piece of your self in the form of blood, sweat, tears, lost sleep and time away from the ones you love. On sale today for $.99!

That little clench you got in your throat?

It's time to get over it.

Ask yourself these questions:

- Do I believe in my work?
- Do I think there is value in my creative output?
- Are there others who have found value in it too?

I find it hard to believe you said no to any of these questions. You may have some doubts, and at times you question yourself. We all have those moments. At your core, you poured yourself into your project, and are ready to share it with the world.

Sales and marketing of your work is necessary and can be fun once you learn to embrace it. Learning to sell yourself, and your work will actually help you become more confident, stretch yourself, and lead to producing better work.

Think about the process of sales this way:

- I introduce new people to my thoughts and words
- Some of those people will enjoy and find meaning in my efforts
- I remind people who already love and enjoy my work that something new is out
- I meet interesting new people, and they love me enough to support me so I can do what I love

No matter who you are, or what you do, someone isn't going to like your product. It's not going to be their taste or style. If everyone was the same, the world would be boring, wouldn't it? Put aside those who aren't your customers, and focus on your followers, your tribe.

☐

4: Operations

What's the Structure of Your Business?

"I wanted to be an editor or a journalist, I wasn't really interested in being an entrepreneur, but soon I found I had to become an entrepreneur in order to keep my magazine going." — *Richard Branson*

The structure of your business will be determined by your goals, business model, and personal financial structure. Each has its own benefits and costs. Depending on the business activities you engage in you may even have multiple businesses, each with its own company structure.

Reasons for doing this include:

- Partnerships for specific projects or businesses
- Protecting personal assets or other businesses in the event a business fails
- Taking advantage for tax purposes or to get loans and grants
- Separating unrelated business activities
- Rebranding.

Depending on what country you are in, there are variations on all the structures below, but these are based on United States law:

- Sole Proprietorship: This is your most likely structure, especially when you are just starting out. Your revenues and expenses flow through your personal income.
- Partnership: If you are involved in certain types of joint projects, or in a small partnership, all members share the revenues and expenses based on their partnership split and percentages. There are multiple forms of partnerships.
- Limited Liability Company: A special form of business structure with the tax benefits of a partnership but gives the legal and financial protections of a corporation.
- S-Corporation: A full corporate structure featuring the protections of a corporation, but revenues and expenses flow through your personal finances.
- C-Corporation: A full standard corporate entity. Financial statements and tax returns are filed separate from the owners.
- Cooperative: A specific type of legal entity where all of the members have ownership and receive specific benefits from the organization.

A good resource for more information on the different business structures, including current changes to financial and tax law can be found with the Small Business Administration. **https://www.sba.gov/starting-business/choose-your-business-structure**.

If you are investing significant assets, generating healthy revenues, or have high expenses, it is usually worth engaging a business consultant, accountant, CPA or attorney to assist you and keep you out of trouble.

For most of you, you will be a sole proprietorship, partnership, or possibly an S-corporation. Only make it as complex as it needs to be and consult an expert if you have questions.

License and Registration Please

Depending on your location and business structure, you may need one or more types of licensing. The most common would be having business licenses and permits based on your place of business. (As an independent or freelance author, editor, or other service provider, you may not be required to have a license or permit, or if you are working directly for an existing business.) More complex business structures, including partnerships, are more likely to require a business license, especially if you look to have specific insurance or separate tax ID's for your business. Check with your local government to determine what, if any licenses you require.

I suggest consulting a local attorney to determine your required course of action if you are unsure.

Be the CEO

"Embrace what you don't know, especially in the beginning, because what you don't know can become your greatest asset. It ensures that you will absolutely be doing things different from everybody else."
– Sara Blakely, founder SPANX

Congratulations, you have founded a business and you are also the CEO! Unfortunately, your business does not yet come with stock options or a golden parachute. At the same time, you are also the Product Development Manager, Vice President of Sales, and Chief Bottle Washer.

What is important is that you are the business, and you need to run it with the mindset of being the CEO. You are in charge: it's time to act like it.

But what do I mean by being the CEO, and having that mindset? It's the difference between having a job and owning a company. Your approach will be somewhat dependent on how and why you have the business you do.

If you write as a creative exercise and hope to make a side income, your goal, budgets, and approach will be very different from that of a full-time writer or editor.

As CEO, you are responsible for the creation and quality of your product and its salability in the marketplace. Even if your publisher is managing the covers, editing, and publication process, you should look at them as your customer, not your employer. They buy your product, package it, and sell it to others. Make sure their actions are consistent with your agreements.

As your business and your career in publishing grows, you should fire yourself from certain jobs, and hand them off to professionals. As we will discuss in this book, there are many roles and jobs related to publishing specifically, such as editors, and agents that you should not attempt as the author of the work. Then there are the functions that exist in every business, like marketing and accounting. These jobs you should evaluate if they are the best use of your time and skills

Once you have hired people, you are also into the management side of being a CEO. You are responsible for the well-being and livelihood of those working for you.

You are also responsible for the overall business strategy as the CEO of your business. What types of material do you want to produce? What genres do you want to edit or produce artwork for? You have to be responsive to the wants and needs of your customers.

Having consulted for a lot of businesses, when dealing with someone who's company is in trouble, I ask, "If you were working as an employee for your company, would you fire yourself for your performance? Or give yourself a raise?" This can be a hard question to ask yourself, and to be critical and honest about how well you are doing. At the same time, you can't be too tough on yourself about things out of your control. We are often our toughest critics. The point of this is to know if you are being the best business owner and creator you can be, and what can you do to become that person.

And last, as the CEO, the brand, and the product, you have the power to be true to yourself. Serve your customers well, and they will do the same for you. As the CEO, President, and Chief Bottle Washer of (insert your name here), LLC, you need to evaluate everything you see, hear, and do as it relates to your business and your brand. You have to consider, how, where, and when to expend your limited resources, while getting paid in the process. Being professional means, you need to understand that your actions and your public presence can affect you, your brand and your business in positive and negative ways.

Flying With the Legal Eagles

The main business of a lawyer is to take the romance, the mystery, the irony, the ambiguity out of everything he touches.
- Antonin Scalia

When starting any business, you know and understand your products or services offered much better than business practices. Part of the reason you bought this book is to get better acquainted with the basics of business.

Outside of accounting, the other great specialty within business is dealing with the legal implications.

I will state for the record, I am neither an attorney, nor am I providing legal advice. I have however had a lot of experience working with attorneys and contracts over the years as a matter of business practice. *The information provided here should not be considered a substitute for legal counsel.*

Contracts and agreements are fundamental to every business. Any time there is a deal between two or more parties, there should be a contract. Get it in writing.

If you ever have a question about a legal agreement, or are unaccustomed to them, I strongly advise working with an attorney in the related specialty. Just like a family physician is not a brain surgeon, a general practice attorney has little or no experience with publishing contracts.

It is better and easier to deal with the questions up front than to discover inconvenient loopholes in the end.

In this section, we will examine the most common legal concerns.

Contracts

As with any business, contracts are the foundation of what you do. Any time you engage with a supplier, a contractor, an agent, publisher, or anyone else providing services or to whom you are providing services, you will need some form of agreement.

Most of the time, these agreements will be boilerplates (a standard legal template for a particular need) which simply state the responsibilities and duties of all parties, and the financial exchange. Contracting someone to print your bookmarks or a sign is normal business practice and you will typically be operating under a simple agreement.

If you are getting into an agreement with an agent, publisher, editor, artist or some other form of partnership, you will want to review the terms and conditions carefully and engage an attorney for independent review. Publishing contracts are infamous for having unique industry terms and conditions.

Note that every contract is just the beginning of a negotiation. Just because someone put a contract in your hands does not mean you have to accept it. Almost any provision is up for discussion.

For example, assume you are selling a short story to an anthology. You will want to make sure to answer these questions (and more):

- How will the work be used and credited?
- Where will it be available?
- What is the period of exclusivity?
- What are the reversion rights?
- What is the compensation model?
- What protections will be used for your work, and the work of other contributors?
- What are your rights regarding your work after the sale?
- What are the rights of the purchaser?
- How will disputes be resolved? Arbitration or legal action? Who is responsible for legal fees?

As always, I suggest having an attorney review any contracts, and in terms of copyrighted work, I recommend using someone who specializes in literary or copyrighted work contracts, and not your family attorney as these contracts typically have some unique qualities.

Intellectual Property

As a creator, you are producing an asset called Intellectual Property (IP). At its core, IP as a legal concept is a unique creation of the mind to which one or more people have the rights of use and ownership. Examples include writing, music, inventions, brands, logos and other forms of art. Legal protections come in the form of copyrights, trademarks, patents and designs.

It is worth noting, it is not the idea protected through IP laws, but the implementation and execution of the idea. You cannot protect the idea of a talking mouse, but you can protect Mickey Mouse vs. Mighty Mouse. Both are anthropomorphized rodents but are developed differently.

Intellectual property can be the result of the work of more than one person. If multiple people are involved in the creation of an idea or work, all involved parties generally have equal rights to the benefits of the IP unless otherwise specified. If multiple people or entities are involved in the creative process, a contract should be used to delineate ownership, and how any benefits from the work will be allocated. It is worth noting, if IP is created by someone for the benefit of an employer, that entity, not the creator, is the primary owner of the product. For example, researchers at a university may have some financial interest in a product they develop, but typically the university retains all rights to use and sell the IP, not the creators. The same is true for businesses doing research and development.

If you are self-employed or are contracted to create a work, that material typically remains with the creator, and the purchaser has limited rights for use. Book covers are an excellent example of this. An artist creating a typical book cover:

- Licenses the rights of the image as a book cover to the author or publisher. Ebook, physical book, dust covers for hardbacks and audiobooks are typically handled as separate licenses or provisions of the agreement.
- The cover rights may include creating SWAG and promotional items given away, but products being sold (such as t-shirts) would require a separate license.
- If the artist uses licensed images from Shutterstock or another company in the creation of the cover, those images carry their own restrictions and licensing agreements which both the artists and purchaser must abide. For example, some cover models will not allow their likeness to be used for romance novels.
- Verify if the license is for exclusive access and use of the specific art and design, or if it may be reused or sold to other entities as a cover, updated only for the title and author's name.
- Having an artist created a branded cover for you may also require agreements restricting your artist's use of your existing styles and trademarks.

Any IP contract should delineate ownership and rights for use of the IP.

Intellectual Property rights can be sold or licensed for use in a number of forms:

- Outright sale of all rights.
- Sale for use for a specific period for a specific limited purpose. An example would be the sale of paperback rights in the United States for a book. The audiobook and ebook rights could be licensed separately.

- Indefinite conditional use is when the rights are sold and belong to the lessee as long as the conditions are met. For example, it could be the exclusive rights of a publisher to a text for as long as one thousand copies are sold per year. Another example would be the lease of a Trademark, conditional to the lessor using it to publish a magazine once per year at a minimum.
- The owner can issue rights under a Creative Commons or similar license.
- The owner can explicitly waive some or all rights to the IP.

In the purest sense, your IP is protected at the moment of creation, but the reality is that it does not work that way in practice. Full protection comes from documentation and filing for the appropriate type of protection (copyright, trademark, etc.) as quickly as possible.

When permitting use of your IP as a part of a business venture outside yourself, make sure you have contracts detailing how any of your work may be used, specific exclusions, and compensation for the use. IP law is highly specialized, and book contracts are a unique morass in and of themselves within IP law. It is best to have any contracts reviewed by someone in the specialty.

In publishing, the first and most common form of rights are those of the copyright. The practice and tradition go back to the Middle Ages where books were hand created and extremely valuable. The owner of the book held the "Right of Copy," meaning someone wishing to reproduce the work would need the permission of the original owner. The first copyright laws were enacted in England in 1710.

Most materials produced by an individual are now automatically copyrighted and protected under US copyright law at the time of creation. Many, but not all countries respect and comply with copyright laws outside of the country of origin. One of the largest violators of copyright law is China (The People's Republic of China or PRC), and if you intend to protect your work in the PRC, it is a separate (and largely useless process for non-citizens of China) copyright registration.

For additional protections, or to pursue legal action concerning a copyrighted work, it must be registered with your copyright agency. As the creator, you are responsible for filing the copyright for any work you are independently publishing. Publishers or others reproducing the work will also typically file the copyright with themselves as the publisher, designating the specific rights of the creator and publisher. Legal counsel is recommended if you are unsure as to filing your own copyright for work sold to a publisher.

In the United States, this is the U.S copyright Office. (Additional information can be found at **http://www.copyright.gov/**.) The cost at the time of this writing is $35, and by default, I register all of my major work.

As a general rule, copyrights for any work created after January 1, 1978 are effective for the life of the author plus seventy years. If multiple creators are involved, the copyright is effective for the life of the final surviving author plus seventy years.

Anonymous works or those written under a pseudonym receive copyright protections for ninety-five years from the first date of publication or one-hundred twenty years from creation, whichever is less. If the owner later registers the work under their own name, the life plus seventy-year rule takes effect.

For work created prior to January 1, 1978, there are different laws and regulations that determine the life of the copyright. If you have a work that falls into that category, such as inherited right, I suggest researching the different laws regarding the date of creation and registration.

Three elements are required to designate the owner of a copyrighted work:

1. The copyright symbol © or the word copyright. It can also be abbreviated as Copr for space constraints.
2. The year of first publication.
3. The identification of the owner or owners, or as they are generally known.

For example, if John Williams publishes under the name of J.K. Smithe, the book, article, or other medium would need to include a notice similar to:

- © 2016 John Williams
- Copyright 2016 J.K. Smithe
- Copr 2016 J. Williams

If you have developed a book, video, music or other piece of IP, additional legal notices may be appropriate on the copyright page of the work:

- Your reservation of rights, and by nature the rights you give to the person possessing the work. You may see the statement "All Rights Reserved," which means the owner of the rights grants no special consideration outside of the possession and use by the individual who purchased the work. Even if not explicitly stated, there is an assumption that fair use is allowed (see the Fair Use Doctrine for more details). The assignment of additional rights or usage will require consent of all partners, publishers, and anyone else with a contractual interest in the ownership and use of the IP.
- Trademark publication notices will be included if there are trademarked IP included in the work (See Trademarks).
- Recognition of the publisher of the work, including name, address, and pertinent information.

- Cataloging and in-publication (CIP is the record of work in process of being published and registered) information will be included if the work is registered with the Library of Congress or other registering entities. This is performed as a part of the registration process and can be done online or in writing.
- Edition or version information so any changes or revisions can be clearly identified.
- The years and publication dates of all printings and releases.
- Recognition of all contributors other than the authors, including editors, designers, proofreaders, and artists.
- Any other bibliographic information that can assist in both recognition of the work and identifying it as original and unique.

As an aside, patents are used to claim ownership of tangibles, items subject to manufacture or creation, or usage of said tangibles. Applications and some other forms of digital media are also subject to patent law instead of copyright.

Some governments (the UK) recognize the separate concept of a design where IP rights of aesthetics, color, and approach are claimed. This can affect cover art, logos, and other distinctions. When doing business, make sure to check the laws and regulations that may govern the transaction and the rights of all involved parties.

To see the current regulations on statutes and limitations, refer to: **https://www.uspto.gov/learning-and-resources/ip-policy/copyright/copyright-basics**.

Creative Commons

In 2001, a new form of protection was created for intellectual property. The Creative Commons License (CCL) was born.
(https://creativecommons.org/)

It is an extension of copyright law and is based on licensing copyrighted material. The CCL is a product of the digital age. It allows people to collaborate, create and make their work available to others in an easy and structured format. You obtain a license for your work and go through a simple process of selecting what and how your work can be used, and what cost if any is associated with that particular use.

Many companies in the technology world get and use CCL as a way of introducing new technologies and charging for the use only if and when the licensor uses it for gain or profit.

For artists and people building businesses, using material created under CCL benefits all. A great deal of music, art, and technology is available via CCL.

As an author and creator of protected work, CCL offers a number of benefits, including:

- Easy and cost-effective tool to allow others to license and use your work.
- Easy and cost-effective tool to find and license the work of others to include in your own pieces (such as music for your podcast).
- The ability to let people conditionally or unconditionally use your work for non-profit or the public good, yet still charge in for-profit situations.
- The Creative Commons organization offers services and counseling on the types of licenses to use and has its own standard licensing agreements content creators can use when offering their IP.
- While the CCL will not cover every situation, it is a viable tool worth considering if you intend to license your IP.

Trademarks

Trademarks are a specific type of protection meant for logos and branding of your business and products. Trademarks apply to any symbol, word, phrase or "trade dress" that distinctively and uniquely identify the manufacturer or the product.

Where you are most concerned in publishing is with your branding. If you establish a particular logo or catch phrase to help identify you and your work, a trademark helps to protect you and your branding.

Trademarks can be established for an individual use through several means but are not granted with the same ease and implicit action as a copyright. Trademarks are first and foremost established by filing for them with the U.S. Patent and Trademark Office (**http://www.uspto.gov/**) or the patent office of your country (if you are outside of the United States). A Trademark can also be awarded if it can be proven that the IP creating the item is "first-use," or proving that you are the creator and innovator of the IP. Having a trademark awarded through the patent office will carry more weight and is typically required for legal action.

Trademarks are designated in several ways:

- TM designates trademarked goods and SM designates trademarked services. ™ designates a trademark earned through the process of regular business. This is the equivalent of earning copyright protection through creation of the work, but carries weaker protections. By tagging your work as ™, it creates a level of expectation that it is distinct and unique to you, and ownership is claimed through the use in business.
- ® designates a registered trademark. This indicates the trademark has been through the full legal vetting and registration process and is recognized by the patent office.

The application process for a Trademark is much more complex than applying for a Copyright as it is much harder to determine if the requested item is distinct and unique enough to not be confused with something else. Due to the complexity of the process, having an attorney with a specialty in Trademark law is recommended.

For most purposes, the TM designation will be more than enough protection for you and your branding.

Fair Use Doctrine

Fair Use Doctrine is a legal principle creating an exception for use of copyrighted material and is one of the few limitations of the IP owner's rights. This is a gray area at best, and refers to the limited ability to "fairly use" content without the permission of the owner.

The doctrine is described in Title 17 of the United States Code, sections:

106 - Exclusive rights in copyrighted works.

106a - Rights of certain authors to attribution and integrity.

107 - Limitations on exclusive rights: Fair use.

Section 107 states:

Notwithstanding the provisions of sections 106 and 106A, the fair use of a copyrighted work, including such use by reproduction in copies or phonorecords or by any other means specified by that section, for purposes such as criticism, comment, news reporting, teaching (including multiple copies for classroom use), scholarship, or research, is not an infringement of copyright. In determining whether the use made of a work in any particular case is a fair use the factors to be considered shall include—

(1) the purpose and character of the use, including whether such use is of a commercial nature or is for nonprofit educational purposes;

(2) the nature of the copyrighted work;

(3) the amount and substantiality of the portion used in relation to the copyrighted work as a whole; and

(4) the effect of the use upon the potential market for or value of the copyrighted work.

The fact that a work is unpublished shall not itself bar a finding of fair use if such finding is made upon consideration of all the above factors. Depending on the usage, you must provide credit to the source to avoid infringement of rights, but this is no guarantee. The doctrine is based on interpretations of case law, which is a dynamic and ever-changing landscape.

You may see opinions that "fair use" exists when content is used not-for-profit, or a sampling of a song is fewer than five seconds. While people look for clear cut rules, they don't exist. There are guidelines, at best. The golden rule is: if you aren't sure, ask permission or license the content.

You can find additional information on Fair Use Doctrine at: (**https://www.copyright.gov/fair-use/more-info.html**).

Public Domain

Intellectual Property in the Public Domain means that it can be used without permission or license by anyone; in essence, works in the Public Domain are owned by all of the public and are not subject to copyright or other protections. In a legal sense, no one owns the exclusive use of the IP, be it a book, film, or other property.

Works can enter the Public Domain in several ways:

- It was created by the United States Government (or other country that excludes its work from copyright law) and is therefore automatically in the Public Domain at creation.

- The Copyright or other protection expires. Copyrights are particularly complex, depending on when the work was created. On January 1, 2019, 1998's Sonny Bono Copyright Act (formerly known as the Copyright Term Exclusion Act) allowed the first mass of copyrighted works to enter the Public Domain in over twenty years, releasing all works published in 1923 into the Public Domain.

- The work was created prior to copyright protections, such as the Bible, mathematical expressions, and the inventions of Leonardo da Vinci.

- Works released without a copyright notice, which after 1978 requires an explicit waiver (the anti-copyright can call notice).

- Issuance of a Public Domain type license which irrevocably grants rights to public use.

Works such as *Sherlock Holmes* is an example of a special case. With series where part of the series is in the public domain, but not the whole, characters and stories that have entered the public domain may be used without permission, but stories and characters not yet in public domain continue to require licensure for use.

Licensing, Use and Misuse of Intellectual Property

It's common that the IP of others is used or incorporated into the creation of new content, as most new creations are derivative innovations. For example, the cover art for a book may belong to another, or elements of licensed images may be included in the work. Also common is quoting original thoughts and text from others in the creation of your new material.

There are many sources of stock images, art, music and video that can be licensed and conditionally used as required. For other content, it is advisable to get written permission or authorization before using it. Outside of a few limitations such as fair use, any time you use the IP of others, their ownership must be recognized. Just like they said in high school and college, quotation without citation is plagiarism. Use of registered work without license is theft.

You should verify if there are any stated or specific restrictions on the use of licensed materials, or you may find yourself subject to legal action.

Here are a few examples of misuse:

- A cover artist used stock photos to create the cover for a romance novel. The specific provisions from the models used specifically stated their faces could not be used any time the included material was of an adult nature. In ebooks, this can be rectified relatively easy, but with printed material it is nearly impossible to recover sold material.
- An artist (A) at an event ran into another artist (B) and discovered Artist B was taking the work of Artist A, repackaging it and selling it as his originals.
- Large sections of language, story lines, and even characters appearing in another's work is a blatant, and unfortunately all too common discovery for many authors.
- A promotional video created for a book series with copyrighted video and music.

Just surfing YouTube for a few minutes will give you more than enough examples of potential violations of the IP owner's rights, even if unintentional. If in doubt about using a piece of copyrighted or trademarked material, I suggest erring on the side of caution. Contact the owner of the work for permission or to license the material.

IP and Your Brand

In a legal sense, your brand is all of the Intellectual Property you own, or the product of your work. Rarely is the challenge to your brand as a whole, it is typically a violation of a specific property, be it a book, a character, or your logo. Other times, a challenge can be an attack on your person or your identity.

As the owner of all of this IP, it can be difficult at times to determine what is a violation of your rights vs. fair use, or even common ideas. (Remember, an idea cannot be protected, it's the execution that is.)

At the end, you have a legal obligation to protect yourself, your company, and all of the pieces of your brand. Failure to do so can put your ownership of those rights at risk as well as your reputation.

What if Your IP Rights are Violated?

What can happen if you violate terms of use for another's IP?

What if someone misuses your IP?

Much of the potential implications will come from how much, if any, money, is generated by the violator or damage is caused by the violation. There are also organizations that aggressively pursue any unauthorized use (I'm looking at you Disney).

- The owner of the IP can demand recognition of the use and ownership.
- The owner of the IP can demand the other party stop specific usage or all use of their property.
- Exceeding the terms of use or going beyond the licensed use can create a new liability for the licensing party (as stipulated in the license contract, if you sell more than 50,000 copies of a book, the cover artist is owed additional royalties).
- The owner of the IP can force the publisher or other delivery agent to cease distribution (such as pulling down a video on YouTube and/or banning the account).
- The owner of the IP can demand and/or sue for damages.

- In certain circumstances, violation of IP can create criminal issues beyond the civil implications.

The severity of the responses to violations also falls back to the owner of the IP. If you discover someone is using your IP for gain (music on a promo video) or is violating the terms of use (such as sharing through torrenting sites) and you do not act, you as the owner of the IP risk losing some or all of your rights and rights to future benefits. Not defending your IP when you know it is being misused or stolen can result in forfeiture of those rights.

The digital world has made it easier to pirate and share work on a global scale. As a general rule (and again, consult an attorney), if you attempt to defend your ownership through sending cease and desist notices, etc., your rights are protected. The process to follow is outlined by the Digital Millennium Copyright Act (DMCA). More on the process can be found here: **https://www.copyright.gov/dmca-directory/**.

Take the level of response warranted by the violation. Seek professional legal counsel as warranted. Also, expect this will take time and money if you elect to take the legal route.

Below is slightly revised reprint of an article I published in 2013 on how not to react to an IP violation.

Piracy Steals More Than Your Work (2013)

As your career advances, you get your work out there, you're more likely to find your work borrowed, plagiarized, stolen, or outright pirated.

Arrrgghhh.

With the exception of a few Luddites and saints out there, we've all done pirated creative work, whether it was copying a song off a friend's CD, ripping a movie from a torrent, or downloading a book. And I hate to be the messenger, but you stole it when you did.

Now that you are a creator of content, it can happen to you too. Once it happens, carefully consider how you react.

If you are friends with or at least follow any number of writers or artists online, you may have already seen someone who's not only had the problem, but has aired it on their blog or all-over social media.

In 2012 when I started seriously writing again, a friend of mine who is a non-fiction writer posted a rant about finding their book being torrented on a file sharing site. Then the second post hit. And the third. After a couple of weeks of daily posts detailing a virtual seek and destroy mission, he'd tracked down some of the people who'd downloaded the work and sent them an invoice.

159

I reached out to him. We had an informal chat where I tried to talk him off the cliff. As I dug in, I discovered it hadn't been going on for weeks, but over two months.

I told him that as a friend and a writer, it is painful and feels like a violation. Then I told him that if he was a client of my consulting practice, I'd tell him he was being an idiot, except the language I used wasn't that nice. (For the record, it didn't go over well.)

After he calmed down and called back, he told me there had been over ten thousand downloads, and the percentage (of royalties) he wasn't getting was nearly $30,000. His advance had been based on five thousand copies and hadn't earned out.

At that time, I made the following observations, and I still think all of them hold true;

- He hadn't written a word on new work in over two months, and was behind on deadlines.
- The public reaction to his social media rants had gone from sympathetic and supportive to one where even his friends and family were tired about hearing about it. He was even losing some of his most ardent fans.
- He has done far more than required to protect his copyright and spent a couple thousand dollars with his attorney in cease and desist letters.
- And most of all, *he probably hadn't lost a dime in sales.*

I sense a number of you out there tensing up on my last statement. My argument is this. Having been in, and around technology for over thirty years, and raised in small business, theft is a cost of doing business. I'm not saying it's right, but locks only keep out the honest and the lazy.

[2018 addendum: In the years since I first posted this article, I have watched at least one person I know do something similar every month. Usually not to this extreme, but still with enough negative effects.]

His long rant stripped away sympathy for the problem, and reduced him to sounding whiny and bitter, costing him customers and readers, and driving new ones away.

Knowing people that regularly torrent movies, music and books, I have a few more observations that are backed by other research:

- A large percentage of material ripped from the internet through file sharing is never seen, heard or read.
- Of those who do consume the material, the ones who enjoy what they find usually also buy the movie or the book, or at least subsequent work.

- Those who aren't going to pay for it never will.
- Print media is not immune. Technology makes it easier and faster than ever to scan and publish printed work. Google got their hand slapped for it.
- Obscurity is a bigger enemy for authors than theft.

Again, I'm not endorsing or condoning piracy, i'm just being a realist. And it may shock you to know that it may not be entirely bad when this happens. Just think, someone thought enough of your material to put it out there in the first place.

Now that we are all aware that some people do not always act legally and ethically, here are some ways to take advantage of the systems and processes that allow for pirating of work (without encouraging it, or doing it yourself).

- Make sure all of your work includes links to your website, social media accounts, mailing list, podcasts, and anything else you can market.
- Solicit reviews at the end of your work. If they are going to steal it, at the least they can leave you a review.
- Use torrenting and other sites to circulate short stories and other platforms to attract followers and drive traffic to you.
- Use the same sites to circulate promotional materials and solicit speaking engagements. Use it for free advertising by circulating short stories and other giveaways.
- Circulate short videos and podcasts publicizing your work, much like you would on social media, within the terms of licenses and agreements.
- Circulate samples of work. I may, one time, have released a copy of a book where it cut off in a pivotal scene, and then had links where you could buy the full copy.

You do have an obligation to protect your rights and your property. In this case it's your work, your art. At the same time, you can't expend so much energy in the process, that you do nothing else. Creators must create. South Park may have given one of the best examples in the episode, "Christian Rock Hard." One side was rampantly successful in spite of itself, and the other side refused to create in fear of theft and streaming.

But the good news is, if you don't produce anything, there's nothing to lose. And no way to gain either.

Arrgghhh, me maties.

Tools of the Trade

"If you don't have time to read, you don't have the time (or the tools) to write. Simple as that."
--Stephen King

The act of writing is a blending of art and technical skills. If you've ever looked at Bibles created during the Middle Ages, they are ornately decorated, and the script is deliberate and precise. It was all hand done. For those privileged few who had access to, much less own these tomes, reading was a sensory experience blending image with the written word.

Since the invention of the printing press, and mechanization of the printing process, every generation has seen leaps forward in the ability to deliver the written word to ever greater audiences. With the advent of computers and the internet and proliferation of smartphones and other mobile devices (especially in underdeveloped nations), almost anyone on the globe has instantaneous access to share thoughts and ideas.

In this section, I'm presenting a sampling of the various tools and technologies available to you. I'm definitely not saying you need them all, or even more than a few. Some may even be obsolete by the time you read this, but I want you to have an idea of what is available. Research and decide what works best for you.

Capturing Ideas

Professionally I am a business and technology consultant. I'm always investigating new tools and technologies for clients and my own interests.

I've participated on a number of panels at events concerning technology for writers, editors, and others in the business. One of the first questions people ask is, "What's the most important tool you use every day?"

I usually say something glib about being the tech guy and hold up an ever-present notepad and pen.

And I use them every day.

The most important tool you have is, of course, your mind. The problem is that all the wonderful ideas bouncing around in there have an expiration date. Sometimes milliseconds, but usually you have a little longer. Inspiration comes from a lot of different sources, but you need to be ready and able to capture any idea. Even that perfectly logical idea to create a self-vacuuming litterbox at 3 a.m. may become a story around the product where the cats in the house use it to assassinate the Shih Tzu.

At 3 a.m., it doesn't have to make sense. Capture it anyway. (I should mention, I don't have cats, and none were harmed in the concept.)

All of that aside, on average I capture thirty to forty ideas a day, even if I'll never use most of them. It could be a story line, a character, a new project, a marketing idea, or even something I need to add to my task list.

There are two stages to this process for me; capture the idea and then figure out if it has meaning or value later.

For the first half, I use several simple tools:

- Pen and notepad - I have a couple of legal pads around my desk, a small pad in the car, one next to the bed, one in my laptop case, and if all else fails, I make notes on napkins and business cards.
- My mobile - In the age of smartphones, I usually either add a note to a running list or e-mail the idea to myself. I have an e-mail address that only I use, and I use it for ideas.
- My computers - I have a desktop and a couple of laptops, all of which sync using Google Drive. I've got several Word documents and Excel spreadsheets to grab and catalog ideas.
  - Scrivener - I have a long list of note cards in different docs.
  - Evernote on both my phone and computers as a cloud-based tool.
  - Google Docs - If all else fails, I've got a running Google Docs page running and add the notes there.
  - Excel workbooks – the great repository (see the details below).

Once a week or so, I embark on the second half of the process, which is to decide what I keep or purge.

If it's a story idea, I've got a couple of different Excel workbooks. Depending on the genre and topic idea, I put in into the workbook that fits best, and spend a few minutes fleshing out the idea and storyline. If I can't work something out in a few minutes, I have an orphaned ideas file where it goes to (usually) die. Every once in a while, an orphan gets a good home.

If it's an idea for a fictional character, they go into another workbook where I already have a pre-built template. I fill it out as best I can, and come back to if I need someone. If it's for a specific project already in the works, I'll add it to the project workbook, and the Scrivener file (more about that later).

Research topics wind up in a pile all their own. If I've heard about a new technology, an interesting piece of history, or just something grabbing my attention, it goes into a file I call the "Rabbit Hole." Sometimes I drop the article or a note onto social media to see what comments it draws. I set time aside to dive into that pile every day, and if something triggers an idea for a client, it winds up in the folder associated with that work. If it triggers a piece for a book project, it either goes into the Scrivener file for the project, or into a working spreadsheet I have for interesting ideas.

The point is, if you get an idea, write it down as best you can and work it later. If it seems it still has merit after a cooling off period, run with it.

I'm going to give you a little insight into my process of developing a book project. I'm not advocating my approach! But since this question comes up frequently, I'm giving it as a point of reference as we move forward. I'm always trying new things and refining my approach, but I'm pretty comfortable with what I do these days.

I'm going to use this book as an example.

1. For years, I've collected a plethora of notes and ideas and assembled them into an Excel spreadsheet.
2. I pulled out several business plans I'd done for clients, both for writing/speaking engagements, as well as other entrepreneurial enterprises, and condensed them to a model that made sense.
3. I analyzed my own processes, not only in developing a book, but also my process for working with clients. I treated myself as a client and consulted for myself in a brainstorming session. The output was a high-level outline in MS Word. I shared it with a few writer friends, a couple of non-writer business partners, and refined the outline.
4. I compared my outline to my notes, reconciled the gaps I had between material and topics that needed research.
5. Research and interviews galore. I read the work of and interviewed other consultants with various expertise, talked to other writers, and used any and every means of information gathering at my disposal.
6. I set up a new project in Scrivener based on the outline and created the research folders I'd have to keep.
7. I laid out spreadsheets brimming with research material and tied those pieces to chapters.
8. I pulled in relevant article and blog posts and articles I'd written over the years.
9. I wrote the first draft in Scrivener.
10. The book sat for three months (while I worked on other projects).
11. I did my first round of self-editing and rewrites.

12. I exported the first draft into Word, did a little formatting, and circulated it among test readers.
13. TI took the feedback, restructured the book in Scrivener, and added new content.
14. Another round of reviews based on the exported version in MS Word.
15. From there, the team and I did all of my versioning, editing and formatting in MS Word. Lots of editing and revisions.

I've been using Scrivener for the last few books and have found it useful to assemble research and to structure books. Moving rough drafts to MS Word for editing and formatting has worked well for me. The change in tools helps me make a mental shift from a development and writing mode into an editing and formatting mindset, as I move away from the tool that has my drafts and research into one with better tools for graphics and layouts. I have also been experimenting with Evernote as an alternative to Scrivener. Each has its strengths and weaknesses.

Letting the manuscript sit for a period before I revisit or do any material editing may seem counter-intuitive, but it an important step in my process. An article usually sits for a few hours to a day. A short story a few weeks to a month. A novel takes around three months. While you can never see your own work with truly fresh eyes, a matter of time and distance gives you a fresh, less biased view of the work.

This is what has worked for me. Time and experience will help you work out your own system. What is important is to find what works for you.

Writing Environment

You may not consider where you write a tool, but the environment in which you're working can have a great deal of influence on your style, content and level of productivity. There are distractions at every turn, be it the laundry that needs to be done at home or a couple having their first date behind you in the coffee shop. How can you make the most of the time you have?

I have a dedicated office in my house and do a lot of work from there. As I write this, I have a desktop, three laptops, an old iPad, an Android tablet, and an iPhone in reach. My scanner and printer are behind me, and bookcases line two walls. On the other side are a couple of whiteboards, a giant pad on an easel, and my desk is buried in books and notes.

When things are busy, or I'm rolling, this is the most productive place for me. I do better when I'm pushed and have a lot going on. If it's too slow, I have too many distractions within easy reach.

It's no surprise that social media, while a great tool, can also suck time into a black hole. Once it's gone, there's no getting it back.

For me, changing environments gives me new perspective and energy to my work much like changing tools between writing and editing. When I'm editing, or planning a project for a client, or even taking calls, my little fortress of solitude keeps me on task. But if I'm writing or trying to be create (be it a client's business plan or a sci-fi novella), I like to get outside around people. The energy, movement, and background noise add a realistic feel and life to the final product.

When I traveled forty-eight weeks a year, I learned to be able to work almost anywhere—airports, planes, hotels, and one time for three weeks, from the top of a filing cabinet. To be clear, just because I can doesn't mean it's the best solution.

By nature, most writers are solitary creatures, at least when they are creating. For me, sometimes being surrounded by others and the living energy of the moment helps sculpt the scene. For me, this is true whether I'm creating fiction or non-fiction. The tangential connection to others reminds the author (us) there really is an audience out there. Plus, you never know when someone's actions can inspire a thought, a character, or even a warning for others.

Even the driest technical writing can benefit from a change in environment; from a cube farm to conference room and active discussion. Circulation of energy inspires more movement of thought within the individual. I never realized how true this was until I pulled a client out of their house to a moderately busy pub and had them write. The change in style and power of writing was astounding to both of us.

At the same time, the wrong environment destroys creativity, like the time a couple broke out in an argument in the restaurant in front of my booth. Or every time (someone who shall remain nameless) brings up Marvel versus DC at a writer's night (even if it's fun).

Your environment can be the most important tool you have in the process, just make sure you can take the rest of your toolkit with you.

Going Digital

With very few exceptions, if you're going to be anywhere in the publishing game these days, you're working with and producing digital media. Yes, there's some satisfaction to clacking away on a manual typewriter, or writing your manuscript in ornate calligraphy, but at some point, it's got to become an organized morass of ones and zeros.

How you get there depends on you. Your budget, your level of comfort with technology, and your general style will all come into play. I've used all of the tools I'll talk about here to at least some extent, but this should be a primer for you to start research on your own, or visit the **https://AuthorEssentials.net** site for tips, tricks, and with your questions.
. There are new tools and technologies being developed every day.

- *Microsoft Office* has set the standard for computer based "productivity tools." As a writing and editing platform, MS Word files (.doc or .docx) are the submission formats most publishers and agents use. Using MS Excel as an outlining and gridding tool during planning and development works well. MS Publisher and MS PowerPoint are invaluable in developing presentations and marketing materials for your work. MS OneNote works well to capture and collate notes from meetings, interviews, and research. And all of them integrate together well. There are also a lot of add-on tools from Microsoft and third parties. The down side is MS Office can be expensive, and Microsoft frequently makes changes that can mess up formatting in older files and documents. Office 365 is part of the migration to cloud-based solutions requiring a near perpetual internet connection.

- *Apache Open Office* is a tried and true open source alternative to MS Office, and the best news, it's free! Writer is your word processor (MS Word), Calc is the spreadsheet (MS Excel), Impress for presentations (MS PowerPoint), Draw is a graphics engine (MS Paint, MS Visio), Base is a database (MS Access) and Math is a tool designed to let you create complex equations to pull into your other documents. I've used all of these tools and have been impressed as Open Office's robustness rivals most of what you can do with MS Office. There are a few shortcomings. The appearance is and user experience is not as refined as Office, most MS Office add-ons will not work with it, and it still can't do everything MS Office can, but for most users it is a powerful alternative, especially for the price.

- *Google Docs* offers Docs, Sheets, and Slides as their alternative to the MS Office suite. They are free as part of your Google account, but the down side is they are browser-based. The up side is the ability keep the documents in the cloud to easily share with co-authors, editors, researchers, etc.

- *WPS Office* offers word processing, spreadsheet, and presentation functionality for Android devices.

- *Scrivener* combines word processing, outlining, research notes, document management and other tools designed as the writer's platform. For the low cost, it's a powerful tool designed specifically for writing, and has templates for many types of projects. You can structure your research materials, including embedding links to online resources inside the project, develop your outline, and even have a virtual corkboard for notes and ideas. Like any robust tool, it takes some time to get the full benefits. Even now, I'm always finding new features. As a personal preference, I find the tools in MS Word better for editing.

- *Evernote* is a cloud-based tool, but its local application includes a word processor, note taking system, organizer, planner, and template system. It excels if you are collaborating with others, and integrates with many tools.

- *Dragon Naturally Speaking* is an adaptive dictation tool that will take your live or recorded speech and transcribe it. I've tried the native speech-to-text applications on the Windows, Apple and Android platforms, but keep coming back to Dragon for its superior speech recognition and features. I've dictated blog posts, and even the entire first draft of a novella with Dragon, but I find it most helpful when doing dialogue. I can dictate directly into MS Word, or I can record it on my smartphone, plug it in, and let the magic happen. It also gives me a way to keep working when I have a thought and want to get it all out faster than I can type.

- *Vellum* is a Mac-based tool for formatting, layout and final production for physical and ebook formats. Scrivener offers many great formatting features, but now exports into Vellum to create superior final results.

- *Scribus* is about the look of the final product over general word processing. It's designed for publication work and competes with Adobe InDesign. I use it with clients to produce event-related materials and for some smaller targeted promotional work.

Beyond this list, there are many more alternatives, especially in the Android and iOS markets, and cloud-based tools. New ones come out every week. I have tested and used others including Novlr, Hemingway, and Ulysses III, but kept to the list of tools I commonly use. Matching the right tools to your writing needs is key to enjoying the process. The good news here is that most of them either feature a free demo version or trial period when there is a cost for the full version.

Research and Planning

Most projects of any size require research, or at least notes and outlines. Even if you are a "pantser," at times you make notes about ideas. For "planners," having outlines and structured notes is critical to success. I float in between.

Other productivity tools can assist with organization, collaboration, and automation of repetitive tasks.

- *Evernote* is a mobile, cloud-based system for organization, task lists, notes, clipping online material, and archiving for individuals and teams.

- *One Note* is Microsoft's note-taking, organization and collaboration tool. It and Evernote share the same fundamental role, but One Note is better suited for free form notes and compiling material where Evernote has a better experience for online and digital media.

- *Scrivener* features robust note taking, outlining and organizational tools for writing projects, and integrates seamlessly with its word processing features.

- *Slack* is a cloud-based tool for collaboration. It features internal secure chats, task and workflow management, and common workspace tools with tracking.

- *Kyber* offers project management, task assignment, calendars, events, reminders and other features to expand Slack's collaboration tools.

- Trello is a flexible web-based organization, accounting, scheduling and project management tool.

- *If This, Then That (IFTTT)* is a free web-based automation tool with plugins and add-ons that lets you automate tasks, such as creating social media posts, responding to incoming emails, backing up your work, triggering notifications from news sources, and any number of other actions. If you can systematize it, you can probably find a way for IFTTT to help.

- *Zapier* is a workflow automation tool with similar features to IFTTT. I use both, as each has different applications and tools.

- *MS Excel* is designed for keeping lists and doing financials but is also a great tool for outlining books or character sheets.

- *Email* is an easy way to send yourself a note. For example, I have a dedicated email address I use to collect notes or ideas if I don't have a notepad handy or want to grab an image for inspiration. I then use IFTTT to add it to file folders, spreadsheets, or other lists based on the code I put in the RE: box.

- *Cloud based storage (Dropbox, Google Drive, iCloud, etc.)* offers easy and low-cost ways to back up work and share with others. I have and use all three of these, as different tools integrate with different platforms. For example, Scrivener integrates with Dropbox (there can be sync issues because of how Google Drive backs up files) whereas Google Docs uses your Google Drive. My iPhone and MacBook back up to iCloud. The workflow tools can then also back up specific files and folders to specific other drives.

Many of these tools offer benefits both to someone working alone and working in collaboration with others. Setting up a Slack channel with your editor and integrating it with the various tools can keep you in sync with each other, and keep a full history of your communications. Setting up task lists and reminders can ensure projects stay on track, and ensure financial activities are accounted for.

Payment Technologies

If you are selling through a distributor such as Amazon or Barnes and Noble, or you are being paid royalties, you don't have to worry about taking payments. If you decide to sell through your website or sell at events or conventions, you will need the ability to accept debit and credit cards.

It has only been in the last decade that digital payment providers and alternatives to expensive merchant processing systems made it easier to accept cards and do business on the internet. Each option has benefits, but as the technologies mature, we see each of these and other companies providing easy and affordable options to small businesses:

- *PayPal* started under another name in 1998, and its purchase by eBay made it a household name in the early 2000's. Predominantly it's used for online sales.
- *Stripe* serves a similar market to PayPal in handling online transactions.
- *Square* entered the market as a low cost card reader using smartphones as the communication and charging platform. Not charging a monthly fee, this is the go-to solution for most small vendors at events.
- *Apple Pay, Google Pay, and bank specific services* primarily service online, but are making significant advances with brick and mortar merchants.

All of these charge fees, typically a fixed amount plus a percentage of the sale. There are other vendors entering this market, but before trying out an unknown name, make sure they have a trusted reputation. The services you use reflect on the trustworthiness of your brand as well.

Scalability!

Scalability is the practice of determining what it would take to grow (or shrink) a system, process or business based on the needs of the customers and environmental demands.

In one way, authors are well suited for increases in demand for their products. Ebooks and audiobooks do not take up physical space and are supported by large scale infrastructure. Print-on-demand services allow for ordering small runs and individual copies of a book which means not having to order or carry inventory.

Conversely, there is a limitation on how much new material an individual author can create, or appearances they can make in a given time period.

Efficient business owners look for tools and support staff to let them do only the things that they as the visionary and creator can do. For authors, this is creating more, and having genuine engagement with their readers.

As you grow, find tools that work for you, build a team that resonates with you, your style and your needs, and make use of the near infinite tools available.

Plus, it gives you more time for those cat videos.

Social Media

"We all have personal brands and most of us have already left a digital footprint, whether we like it or not. Proper social media use highlights your strengths that may not shine through in an interview or application and gives the world a broader view of who you are. Use it wisely."
- Amy Jo Martin

It seems like a relatively simple question, but let's start with a definition of social media to be on the same page, so to speak.

In the most basic form, social media is any digital platform allowing people to interact (i.e., be social) involving the creation and exchange of information (media) in virtual environments. You will find this definition is vague and allows for a lot of leeway in determining what actually is social media. Is a blog social media? Your website? YouTube? Online gaming? An online version of a magazine?

In their own way, all of these have elements of social media in them, but are also much more, and we will address those separately.

While I do mention this elsewhere, it is worth remembering each of these different platforms is a business, and its first responsibility is to itself and its owners, not you and your needs. Read and understand the Terms of Service when contemplating using them.

I mentioned earlier in social media about a recent change with Tumblr, following actions of Facebook, Twitter and other platforms to "sanitize" the content and tighten the definitions of "potentially offensive" or "inflammatory" content, resulting in the blocking and removal of many posts, and deletion of some accounts. I personally wound up in Facebook jail for a couple of days, being reported for having shared an academic article referring to hazing rituals in ivy league schools from the 1920's due to pictures included in the article and references to abuses at the time.

As platforms increase usage and mature, you will find the terms change, as do the services and their performance. I am going to use Facebook as an example because they are one of the major platforms, and most users are going to be familiar with their changes over time. What Facebook shows in its feeds is based on complex algorithms, matching you, the friends and groups you are linked with, and the company's current strategies. As of the writing of this book, it is estimated three percent of the total average followers or users of any given individual or business will have their posts seen "organically."

Three percent of your friends, customers, or followers will see a given post. In times past, those percentages were much higher, and as a creator you could count on a significant percentage of your posts showing up in a fan's feed. You can still see all of a particular person's posts if you go to their page, but only some will show up in any individual's feed.

Why, you may ask.

It is twofold. First, if you saw every post by every person in your feed, even with a relatively small number of connections, you would be buried in a flood of posts you wouldn't necessarily care about. The algorithms use the people you connect with most, posts you tag with "likes" or comments, and other factors to determine who shows up in your personalized feed. Users can influence their feed by spending a little time interacting with old friends whose posts you haven't seen in a while, sharing and liking the content you as the consumer would like to see more often, and using Facebook's rules to hide and block what you don't want to see.

The second reason should be obvious, but often is not. Social media is big business. People do not consider that most of these services do not charge users and assume the advertisements they largely ignore cover the expenses. This is correct in that the main business of most social media companies is to build a customer base to sell advertising space to sponsors. This means, as a creator and a business, sponsoring content (read, buying advertising, boosting posts) gets you more visibility. But social media companies are also social profiling and social engineering companies as well.

As you build out your social media presence and expand your brand, you are also going to discover that many platforms have relationships with each other, and often share information. This can be both a benefit and a detriment, depending on what you're doing and how you feel about personal privacy. Every like, share, click and connection you make on social media platforms contributes to their profiles of you, what they market to you, and in some cases, how they try to influence your thinking. Facebook in particular has been called out for conducting social experiments on users without their consent.

One final warning, and one I feel sure you will smile about. Manage your social media; don't let it manage you.

Social Media Platforms

As of 2018, seventy percent of the people in North America have at least one social media account. Globally, 2.7 billion people are on social media.

I don't say this to bore you with statistics, you can find plenty of that online on your own. I bring this up for a little perspective on the population of people you can connect with in the virtual universe.

The list of platforms I mention is by no means complete. New ones launch and fall every day, but these tend to be regarded as the major current platforms. It doesn't mean you need to on all of these, or any of them at all. But if you do, go where you feel comfortable and have the best opportunity to connect with your fans, based on your own personal preferences, style, and your products.

- *Facebook* (**https://www.facebook.com/**) is still the largest social media platform and is still generally regarded a must have. For authors, or almost any type of business, it gives a lot of avenues to connect with potential and existing customers and build relationships. It allows you to have your personal page on which to blog and share your message, the ability to create pages for specific products or services, create and host online events, share video, and even have real-time chat. It's also a great place to set up private groups for your street teams and fans.
- *Instagram* (**https://www.instagram.com/**) is a photo and video sharing site. Though it might not seem to be an obvious tool for an author, you can use it to post covers, photos and videos from events, and things about yourself. You never know when a picture of the dog will create a connection.
- *LinkedIn* (**https://www.linkedin.com/**) is a business and professional networking site. It is a good way of connecting with industry professionals, and doing research about services. It's also an excellent resource when building your reputation in a field.
- *MeetUp* (**https://www.meetup.com/**) is not a social media site in the traditional sense but is designed to have people meet (gasp) in the real world. You can find and host groups for almost any purpose to connect with others. It works especially well, for example, to form a writing or critique group. It can also be used to bring attention to events.
- *Periscope* (**https://www.periscope.com/**) is a video sharing website. Much like Instagram, you can share experiences through video.
- *Pinterest* (**https://www.pinterest.com/**) is a digital pin-board site. Like many platforms, it is a good resource to share yourself with others, and good resource for inspiration and connections. Imagine creating a pin-board for each book with the cover and pictures that inspired or reflect different scenes and locales from your story. Pinterest is regarded also as a search engine and a good source for SEO to drive traffic to your site due to their affiliation with Google.

- *Quora* (**https://www.quora.com/**) is a knowledge-sharing site and driven by its contributors, similar to Wikipedia. If you write and are developing your reputation with an expertise, contributing to the knowledge base can help you build your brand and reputation.
- *Reddit* (**https://www.reddit.com/**) is an example of a viral news site. Through Reddit, members create and share content, grouped by areas of interest and foster discussion. I would suggest, however, checking your feelings at the door.
- *Slideshare* (**http://www.slideshare.net/**) is a resource largely used by professionals to share presentations and tips on developing them. If you write or speak on any topics, you may well find a presentation on it, or share your own presentations to gain an audience. It is also an excellent resource for ideas and information.
- *Snapchat* (**https://www.snapchat.com/**) is an imaging and messaging service. It can provide a great platform for connecting with friends and fans, communicating while at events, or other activities you want to share with your fan community. At current, posts have a limited life span and expire quickly, creating short term conversations, but the company may start allowing opt-in for posts to live longer.
- *Tumblr* (**https://www.tumblr.com/**) is a blogging and microblogging resource.
- *Twitter* (**https://twitter.com/**) is a microblogging resource, connecting you with fans 280 characters at a time. It supports linking to other platforms, sharing images and videos in posts. Combined with Tweetdeck and hashtags, you can host threads and conversations.
- *YouTube* (**https://www.youtube.com/**) is a video streaming site. It can be an excellent resource for research as it's a search engine, but you can also drive traffic by posting videos advertising your work, products, and services. If you are a speaker, you can also treat it much like a video podcast, build subscribers and a follower list. Owned by Google, content tends to rank higher in searches.

In addition to the sites above, there are a number of platforms dedicated to books and literature. Many will allow you to create author pages, links to your books and where to buy them, and allow people to add reviews. Some of the most popular are:

- *Goodreads* (**https://www.goodreads.com/**) is currently owned by Amazon, but has not completely integrated with the retailer side. It has one of the largest communities, and allows you to share not only your work, but what you are reading and your literary interests as well.

- Library Thing (**https://www.librarything.com/**) classifies itself as a Book Lovers Community. From an author perspective, it is a direct connection with readers.

- Scribd (**https://www.scribd.com/**) is a service dedicated to delivering ebooks and audiobooks but allows the authors and artists to connect with readers as well.

- Wattpad (**https://www.wattpad.com/**) leans more towards connecting authors and readers and gives prospective authors a chance to test drive work and find readers before publication.

This is only a sample of the platforms available to you as an author but lists the heavy traffic sites and a few niche ones as well.

If you want current statistics, the Global Web Index survey (**http://insight.globalwebindex.net/social**) is a valuable resource.

Advertising with Social Media

There are two major approaches to advertising via social media: organic and paid.

Organic growth and organic advertising are descendants of the oldest and best form of advertising: word of mouth. Except now, word of mouth often comes through people connecting electronically. In the earliest days of the internet, news traveled through bulletin boards and newsgroups which were the social media of their day. When platforms such as Myspace and later Facebook became popular in the early 2000s, it benefitted both the users and the social medial companies to encourage organic advertising. Everyone gained exposure and an audience. Younger platforms still use this approach today.

The good part of organic advertising is that it is free and best propagated by your true fans and followers. At times, you may be part of a message or it may be a meme that goes "viral" and gains a lot of attention.

As with all businesses, they have to change and grow as their business does. And with a few exceptions, they are not non-profit organizations. As social media companies mature, they tend to change their models and algorithms making it much harder to have organic growth. They generate revenues through paid advertising. Whether this means purchasing banner ads, boosting posts, or any number of other paid services, to increasing the exposure of your business will take some investment.

Today, your marketing strategy should take advantage of organic where it can, but with the knowledge that well-invested advertising can reap significant returns. Refer back to the section on Marketing Plan.

Nineteenth-century merchant John Wanamaker is credited with saying, *"Half the money I spend on advertising is wasted; the trouble is I don't know which half."* No one knows what will work and what will not. You also may never know exactly what combination worked and why, even though you may have strong ideas. You should also keep in mind that the business environment changes quickly, and what worked last year may need to be adjusted or tossed into the recycle bin.

Even the largest corporations have failed campaigns. It can be something like New Coke where the company didn't understand what their customers wanted of their brand and product. McDonald's brought back Szechuan sauce for a single day because of the Rick and Morty TV show, and underestimated demand to the point of near riots. Even worse, linking your brand and product with pop culture and current events can be risky. Kendall Jenner's Pepsi ad tying in to the Black Lives Matter movement and the ensuing backlash was a huge blunder. Compared with the bump Oakley received by providing sunglasses to trapped miners after their rescue, it is a matter of timing and good taste. If you really want to get sucked down a rabbit hole, there is some value in researching "marketing campaign failures."

Through networking, using advertisers, publicists, agents, and other professionals, you can develop and profit from your marketing strategies.

There's an App for That

The societal transformation smartphones and tablets have brought since 2007 has also revolutionized business for authors. Audiobooks, convenient e-readers, and even social media in the palm of your hand at all times means we can read, write, record, and interact any time, any where.

Most social media platforms developed their own apps optimized for the devices and some platforms like Snapchat are only available only through mobile devices.

As of this writing, here are applications to consider and how they may be used as a part of your business:

- Facebook strives to be the premiere mobile tool, offering not only the ability to post and share content, but also text, voice, and now video messaging. Facebook Live puts video streaming and broadcast technologies in the everyone's hands. This gives a number of tools for connecting and networking with friends, colleagues, other industry professionals, service providers, and customers. At events, you can provide live updates and information to others who may be there or share the experience with those who are not.
- Twitter's mobile application gives access to the full abilities of the microblogging platform and using hashtags (#) allows for group conversations, pictures and short videos in real time.
- Periscope, which was bought by Twitter, allows you to record and share short videos, that are kept and shared with followers for twenty-four hours.
- Instagram (bought by Facebook) offers Instagram stories and the ability to create short linked videos to create a full narrative.

Crowdfunding

One of the interesting features of social media is a particular niche of crowd-sourcing and crowd-funding. Crowd-sourcing is the act of reaching out to a community at large, typically through digital means, to research information, gather materials, or recruit people and resources for a particular task. It has become popular as a tool in the open source community for developing applications and tools.

For the personal and small business community, crowdfunding has arisen as a way for large numbers of people to contribute to projects and causes. As a resource, crowdfunding has a number of potential benefits:

- It can raise significant funds from contributors around the planet from very small to very large amounts, and quickly.
- During a period of fundraising, it can be used to bring awareness through social media to a given project as an advertising engine.
- It can be used to pre-sell products and services.
- It is a relatively low-risk way to test interest in a product before significant work or investment.
- Investors are more likely to come from or become loyal customers and true fans.
- It is possible your project could "go viral" and achieve a high level of organic marketing attention. Due to the nature of crowdsourcing, it often benefits existing investors to have others buy in to make sure a project is funded or to reach stretch goals.

- If you receive enough attention through crowdsourcing, it may bring more traditional forms of investment as well.

The platform you choose can have a big influence on your being successful. Read and understand the Terms and Conditions before starting any campaign. When preparing to pursue crowdfunding, there are risks and factors to consider:

- Crowdsourcing campaigns often run for a fairly limited period, meaning you need to generate interest quickly. Typically, you want to start generating interest before the campaign begins. The first twenty-four hours can often determine the success of a campaign.
- If your campaign does not fund, you may not receive any funding and yet be liable for fees. Review the terms and conditions carefully to understand the consequences of not meeting your goal.
- Unfunded projects can also affect the reputations of those involved, depending on the reason for failure or withdrawal of the project.
- Ensure you have legal protections of Patents, Trademarks, or Copyrights in the event someone steals the idea from a failed project.
- Ensure you can deliver on any rewards offered in the event of unexpected levels of success. There are many cases where campaigns were spectacularly successful to the point where the project team struggled or was unable to deliver as promised (The Exploding Kittens game).

The strategy you use for crowdfunding can vary depending on the platform, but there are consistent components to the plan:

- Drive as much traffic to your project as possible through your mailing lists, social media, and any opportunity that presents itself.
- Invest in your campaign to attract interested parties. This means advertising, solid copyrighting, promotional videos and materials.
- Have consistent and clear communication with your investors about good news and bad. If due to overwhelming response you will not be able to fulfill the project as promised, be honest. If there are unexpected challenges, communicate them and your plan for resolving them.
- Stretch goals can incentivize people to market your project for you.
- Be clear on how much you need and what people will get for their investment.
- Treating your investors well for one project will bring them back for future projects.

If you consider crowdfunding for your project, it is worth noting not all sites are the same. There are a multitude of business models, and they service customers in a number of ways. The list below is representative of some of the many platforms and gives you an idea of the available options.

Crowdfunding Platforms Quick Reference

Crowdfunder	Website	Use for	Fees	All or None?
Kickstarter	www.kickstarter.com/	Excellent for creative projects and enterprises, one of the largest communities	8-10%	Yes
IndieGogo	www.indiegogo.com/	General model with fixed and flexible goal models	6-12%	No
Patreon	www.patreon.com/	Directed towards recurring payments and ongoing support	11 - 16%	No
RocketHub	www.rockethub.com/	Targets Art, Business, Research and Social projects	6-12%	No
GoFundME	www.gofundme.com/	Mostly for personal needs and use, or for funding projects at a local level	7-8%	Yes

Your Social Media Business PSA

2018 was the year many people received a hard and fast education about Social Media. The number one lesson? Security and social blend like oil and water. Among the many companies that had data breaches, or more often, people discovered that these companies sell your data, Facebook wound up in a list of headlines and in front of congress. I'll say it again; don't post something you don't want to see again in the future.

The other lesson, and the one I believe to be more important, your social media presence is not your real estate. It's leased at best, and a profit center for someone else always. We saw many people who were making their living as internet famous have their Facebook, Twitter, YouTube and other platforms disappear overnight for violations of the "terms of service." In other cases, content that had been acceptable was now being stripped as offensive.

I will use Tumblr as an example.

Romance writers found that having two half naked men on the cover of a book was no longer acceptable. One was still fine, as long as the object of affection was of the opposite sex. LGBTQ, environmental, political, and other content was deemed to be unacceptable for their users.

Overnight.

Blogs, videos, and posts with years of content were just gone without warning.

I cannot emphasize enough that social media platforms are companies that exist and operate for their own benefit, and their user communities influence the rules and policies of these organizations. This means an individual or community can be deemed unacceptable or offensive by a relatively small and vocal group, and the platform respond to its users.

We are encouraged to use and build followings for ourselves and our work using these platforms, and often spend hundreds of hours a year or more doing so. But understand, this is not your real estate, and the rules are theirs to change. If your entire business and career is built on these platforms, it can be gone tomorrow. It may be that the platform shuts down, or that they simply shut you down.

Build as much of your business on the real estate you own and control, your website and your email list.

Your Website

The Internet tempts us to think that because an email or a new website can be accessed in seconds that everything works at the same instant speed. Art is more like the growth of a plant. It needs time and space.
- Stephen Hough

In any business today, it is an expectation you will have some sort of digital presence. With almost all platforms, you have restrictions and limitations on what you can post and how it appears.

You have a number of options to consider as your "website," and as an author will likely employ many of these.

Social media platforms offer businesses and authors pages to build their online presence and market their products.

- Amazon (https://www.amazon.com/) author pages feature the picture and biography of the author and links to their books. While it has some limitations, it is free and should be a part of your overall digital presence and strategy.
- Goodreads (https://www.goodreads.com/) offers a similar author page as Amazon. Though Goodreads is owned by Amazon and they're linked, they offer separate sites, tools, and customer experiences.
- Facebook (https://www.facebook.com/) uses individual pages which can be liked to your profile. Facebook ads are based on pages. You can build pages as an author and dedicated pages for each book or series, and post information specific to it. Consider Facebook Groups part of this environment as well. Both open groups and closed ones for your street teams.

Other social media platforms offer similar ways to build an information page. While you have some control over these platforms, you are still subject to the Terms and Conditions of the platform, and their business practices.

Beyond this is the ability to create your own individual website. This can be done for free, but I do recommend paying a little to have your own domain and e-mail address.

But why do you want your own website? Why do you need one?

By now, you've probably said, "I just want to write" about a hundred times. An hour.

Having your own website lets you do exactly that. You get to write and put up anything and everything you want. I'm not saying that is always a good idea, but it is the one place you can absolutely control (almost.) As long as it is legal, you have the ability to put it up. Social media is no replacement for having your own website. This is virtual real estate you own. You control the appearance, user experience, content, and the rules. With a few exceptions, no one can take it from you. Other than hosting, you are not dependent on a platform staying in business or changing its rules.

A reminder, and a little warning. Your website should represent you, your brand, and your business. Keep it professional. It should represent exactly what you want the world to know about you and your brand.

As we move further into this process, consider what you actually want to put on your website. You can go out and look at different sites in and out of your genre and business to see what speaks to you, but there are certain basics your website should have:

1. An About page that includes:
- Your professional biography, and if appropriate some personal background as well.
- A headshot or picture helps people connect with your bio.
- Awards, nominations, etc.
- Social media links
- Your contact information should be easily available, as well as your agent, publicists and publishers if you have them. I suggest having multiple e-mail addresses, at a minimum one that is public and one that is private for your businesses. I have multiple, each with a targeted use and audience. But make sure people can get in touch with you in a safe manner. I also suggest having one used just for signing up for mailing lists to manage incoming email traffic. If you want to post a mailing address, get a Post Office Box. Do not post your home address.
2. A Published Works page, including:
- A list of all of your works.
- Links to major retailers for each, including formats (hardback, paperback, ebook, audiobook.)
- A page or sub-page for each series or type of work.
- Links to reviews.
- Post a couple of your best or most noticeable reviews.
- Badges for nominations and awards.

3. Your Blog:

- You're a writer. A blog is an easy way of connecting with people, while doing that thing you want to do most: write. You can talk about yourself, what you are doing, where you have been, work in progress, just about anything you want. You never know when the story about your cat dressed like Don Quixote riding on a Roomba could go viral. Odds are, if your cat caught a chipmunk and put it in your bed, it won't go viral, but might get you a little sympathy. One nice feature of blogs, you can post other people's work to your site (attributed to and/or with their permission), and they can do the same with yours. Blog tours are an excellent way of gaining visibility and help everyone involved.

4. Your Calendar:

- If you do appearances or events, your calendar should tell your fans where to find you and meet you. Sign their books. Sign their iPads. Sign a napkin, if that is what they want. I do have a few lines about what I'll sign, but very few. By profession, I am a consultant, and morally flexible.

5. A Contact form:

- In addition to your "About Page," you should have a basic form that lets people send you notifications and requests. As a rule, you would want fields for name, email address, and a free form area for the message. If you do custom work, you may have specialized fields for gathering additional information.

6. A Mailing List form:

- Your mailing list is the only form of active contact and advertising you will own. As mentioned in Building Your List, you should be collecting names for your mailing list, including making it easy for people on your website to join. If you aren't yet cultivating your mailing list, start today.

7. Media/Press Kit:

- If you do or wish to do conferences and media appearances, having a quick and easy media kit with information about you, your biography, a head shot, press release, testimonials, your presentation summaries and speaking interests prepackaged expedites your applications.

8. Social Media Links:

- Links to all of your social media profiles should be readily available for people to connect with you, follow you and share your latest blog post. Links and buttons should be easily accessible and encourage people to help spread your reach.

Your website content and design should be tailored to reflect you, your work and your style to showcase your products, and the value they bring.

As you design your website (or have someone do it for you), have an intention behind every part. The buttons, pop-ups and instructions you give are referred to as "calls to action." Make it clear and easy for people to understand what you want them to do while they are on your site, be it signing up for your newsletter, following you on social media, or buying your latest book.

Pick Your Platform

Once you have considered what will feature on your website, the next question becomes which platform to use. There are several approaches you can take to building your website.

Starting at the most basic level, one of the easiest ways to build a site with a minimum of technical experience is to create a WordPress site at Wordpress.com. You are also limited in being able to link to or sell products through your site, and have few options in terms of the plugins and features you can use. Creating a site is free to you, but the sites are paid for by the host with advertising you do not control, and may detract from or conflict with your brand and products. In addition, the ads on your site may have nothing to do with your content or even be inappropriate for your audiences. I recommend hosting your own site to get the maximum control and benefits that it offers.

WordPress powers over 30% of all websites and growing as of 2018 and is available for free download at wordpress.com to load it onto your own host and domain. Tens of thousands of themes and plugins allow you to create professional websites.

The next two closest competitors combined are just a fraction of that.

Is being the biggest player enough reason to use it?

On its own as an argument, no. Here are my reasons for using it. Do your own research and make up your mind (and remember, depending on when you read this, conditions may have changed.):

- The FREE options are powerful and look great.
- WordPress is a universal platform that can be migrated and used on almost any hosting solution, and most hosting companies will install basic WordPress for you. People are accustomed to seeing WordPress sites and are used to doing business on them.
- It is easy enough for a non-technical person to get a basic site and blog up and running, but powerful enough for Fortune 100 corporations to use for their businesses.
- Natively, it is a Content Management System (CMS). This means it helps you manage your content, be it the blog, your calendar, or the products your business sells. If you change hosting or domains, it's easy to move without losing your site, content, and SEO.
- Natively, WordPress is an excellent blog engine, as that's what it was originally developed to be.
- There are thousands of "themes" available to create the look, feel, and framework for your site.

- Plugins are available to support almost any feature you would like to include in your site. (Note: Most plugins and themes are not supported on Wordpress.org, the free hosting site) This includes plugins for almost every social media platform, payment gateways, mailing list services to inventory and customer databases. If you want to do it, there is probably a plugin for it. Complete eCommerce solutions have been built just for the WordPress framework.

- Using RSS, it is easy to share your blog, and has excellent functionality allowing people to re-blog your posts to their own WordPress sites.

- It is designed with SEO (Search Engine Optimization) in mind, which means your site and your content is easier to find.

- It's safe and secure, and WordPress releases regular updates, many of which are security features.

- It handles almost any media you need, from posting pdf's to running embedded videos.

- If you need customization work done, it is easy to find support.

Even with all of the positives, WordPress isn't the only platform I've worked with or use. For the purposes of most anyone reading this book, it's my first choice, and I expect it will be for some time.

Now that I have given you option A, we will look at a few other options:

You can use a service that hosts and provides a pre-built template such as WIX.com or Squarespace.com. For video content and workshops, I use Kajabi. On the plus side, these tend to be easy to use, but can be costly and limiting in style, design, and functionality. Also, if you decide to move hosting services, you will be starting from scratch with your website, lose your history and your SEO ranking.

In lieu of WordPress, you can consider these platforms:

- Concrete5 (https://www.concrete5.org/) is an open source content management system with a lot of support for SEO and native information capture capabilities, and support for Marketing activities.

- Drupal (https://www.drupal.org/) is a content management system similar to WordPress. In addition to blogging, it supports forms, creating levels and tiers of content, and a wide range of content structures. It has an excellent user community for support and is more flexible in building website structures.

- Joomla! (https://www.joomla.org/) is a powerful open source content management (CMS) platform. Basic websites are relatively easy to get up and running. If it had a down side, the complexity and power is greater than most creators need. Like Drupal, it is often used for large and commercial sites, but works well for most uses.

- SilverStripe (http://www.silverstripe.org/) is similar to WordPress and provides a lot of flexibility and support for SEO. On the down side, there aren't as many themes and modules to add functionality.

These are only a few of the options available, and you will find commonalities between them. Depending on your goals and needs, there are many options to get your website up and running for any budget from free, to "the sky is the limit." (If you have an unlimited budget, call me. Let's talk. Even if you don't we can help.) We will dive into this deeper, but I strongly suggest registering your own domain name, having separate website and e-mail hosting so that you have complete control and ownership.

What's in a Name?

You have gotten past the first step and decided what you want to do with your website, and picked a platform to put it on.

The next key consideration is to determine what to call your website. While you can label it anything you like, you want for the domain name to be easy to use and remember.

What is a domain name? It is the nice and easy name you use in a web browser to point to your website (for example, google.com, authoressentials.net, or yourauthorname.com such as **http://www.jim-mcdonald.net/**, one of the names I write under).

They are governed through the Domain Name System (DNS), and can be acquired by going through a Domain Name Registrar. Most website hosting companies also have the ability to register a domain for you.

You of course may have to come up with a few options in the event your first choice is not already owned by someone else. You can check various domain names by going to any domain service, but an easy one to use is **https://www.whois.net**. I am both a registrar with my own service and have used **https://Namecheap.com** to register my domains. If the domain is owned by someone else, you can offer to purchase it. Sometimes you will find a price listed, other times you have to make an offer.

If you find your preferred domain is taken, I suggest trying a different name for ease of use and cost. Also note, if you search for a domain and have any interest in using it, register it quickly or you may find someone has bought it and parked on the site in the hopes you will come buy it from them. (A domain can cost less than $1 a year or run into the hundreds, depending on the extension. Website URL's ending in .com and .net are usually less than $15 per year, if they are available.)

A few considerations for your domain name (and I have broken them all, and paid the price of admission):

- Do not use hyphens (such as **http://jim-mcdonald.net**) as they break up the name, and are hard to announce on an interview, from a panel, etc. They also are a pain to type on mobile keyboards. (One of the many lessons to learn from my own mistakes.)
- Do not use numbers as they can confuse the person (Is it JSmith3.com or JSmithThree.com).
- Do not use something that could be misread or misinterpreted because of combining words or letters without spaces (I'll let your imagination run on that one.)
- Do not use a name hoping to mislead people or bring in traffic because people use .com by default vs. .org or .gov, or names that may come from typos (koke.com).
- Do not register your domain through your hosting company, even if they give you a "free" domain. They are bundling the cost into your hosting, but if you have problems with your host, or just need to move it, it can be time consuming and troublesome to get your domain from the hosting company. Any number of times, I've had to help clients through this process, and their website, email, and everything connected to the host can be down for a week or more during the transition, and may run into additional fees to "buy" your domain from them.

Once you have registered your domain, consider using WhoIsGuard (http://www.whoisguard.com/). This is also available through most domain name registrars. This is a service that gives anonymity to and protests the identity of the owner of the site. This is important, especially if you use a nom-de-plume or are otherwise protecting your identity.

Many "free" hosting services, such as Wordpress.org give you a free domain name. It would look something like
"http://YourName.Wordpress.com" or
"http://JSHosting/YourName."
These are hard to use, and don't reflect a unique brand.

If you decide to build your own site and manage it through a hosted solution, they may incentivize you to contract with them for hosting services by including the cost of the domain name (often telling you it's free). This type of domain name is the subdomain to a larger organization, affecting your SEO (Search rankings on Google, etc.) and makes you appear less professional. You also may find some restrictions on what you can do depending on the hosting site if you use their free version.

Whether it is included in the hosting fees or not, I do not recommend having your hosting company also be the registrar for your domain. Some hosting companies will hold ownership of your domain or make it difficult to transfer a domain to a different hosting service. I just went through this process with a client, and the hosting company refused to release the domain name for eight days until it expired, despite having transferred the name to a new source. This resulted in the client's website, email, and everything tied to it being down for eight days, plus the time to configure everything with the new host.

Or they may hold ownership of your domain to make it harder for you to move hosting companies.

As a general rule, hosting starts at $3-$6 per month for your site (see the section on hosting), and registering the domain name can be as little as $.88 a year, *.com names are usually $11 - $15 per year.

As with anything, if you decide to have your website hosted, do your research and read reviews. Cheaper is not always better. A lot of great companies do hosting and provide excellent customer service. There are also several major brands that have reputations for poor customer service at high prices. Also, look for hosting companies with well-developed forums for customers and support if you are doing the work yourself. If you contract out at least the initial construction of your website, your developer may make recommendations for you.

Be a Good Host (Hosting Your Website)

Assuming you decided to host your own website and have selected a platform on which to build it, the next question becomes hosting. Not all hosting, or hosting companies are created equal.

Some hosting companies specialize in a particular platform, and this is especially true of WordPress. Many hosting companies offer services tailored to WordPress, and some exclusively host for this platform.

As you evaluate your options, you will see the iron triangle of balancing cost, service quality, and services offered. You can always pick two of the three, but finding the right balance is up to you.

1. Free Hosting

Depending on what you intend to do with your website and the services you plan to offer, this is often a good starting point. Most free hosting companies offer space with some website designs and template options, in exchange for hoping you drive visitors and ad clicks.

Pro: there are no direct costs to you; bandwidth and page load speeds are usually adequate for low volumes of visitors.

Con: you have no control over the advertising on your site; The advertising may detract from you and your products; you typically have limited options in design, or plugins for functionality; it can limit your SEO and be a challenge when you move or upgrade your site.

2. ***Shared Hosting*** (Recommended for most people)

Shared hosting is when you have space in a server farm with thousands or tens of thousands of other websites.

Pro: Low cost; Full control over your website design and options; Ability to create multiple targeted email accounts for your domain; easy to move hosting services.

Con: Bandwidth and page load speeds tend to be slow; A security vulnerability on someone else's website may pose a vulnerability to you and your site; "Unlimited Bandwidth" as is often seen is a misnomer, you won't be charged for high volumes but the server likely cannot handle mid-tier and high levels of traffic; A DDoS or other attack on another person's website on the same server can affect you and potentially make your site unavailable as well.

3. *Virtual Private Server*

A VPS is a little like a shared server in that you are sharing hardware and processing power, but your environment is limited to you and your domains. I would only recommend a VPS for the more technologically skilled, and those who intend to run more complicated sites, such as for gaming or hosting applications.

Pro: Full control over the environment, including system parameters; Fast bandwidth and page load speeds.

Con: Higher costs; Requires you as the owner to do more system and environmental maintenance.

4. *Managed Hosting*

Managed hosting gives you get the best combination of benefits from Shared Hosting and VPS. You have full control over your site, but the security and administrative tasks are largely handled for you.

Pro: Full control over the environment; Fast bandwidth and page load speeds; More website security, especially for WordPress platforms; ability to handle higher traffic volumes and high-performance needs like podcasting.

Con: Costs start at about triple the cost of Shared Hosted. You as the owner are responsible for almost all maintenance.

5. *Dedicated Hosting*

Dedicated hosting is having your own dedicated server. In the modern movement to cloud based systems, this solution is only a good fit for those running high volume sites with commerce sales, multimedia experience, forums, and other high bandwidth needs.

Pro: Full control over the environment, including system parameters.

Con: Highest Cost; high maintenance needs.

Hosting Scale (1 is lowest, 10 highest)

Hosting Type	Cost	Quality/ Experience	Control/ Services	Ease of Use
Free	1	1	1	10
Shared (Recommended for most uses)	3	4	5	7
Virtual Private Server (VPS)	5	7	8	2
Managed	8	8	8	3
Dedicated	10	10	10	1

For most of my clients, I see them progress from Shared Hosting to Managed Hosting. Many start with the free option, at least until they have built a small following. For the cost and flexibility managing your own site gives you for the potential benefits, I only suggest using the free option for hobbyists and people not looking to generate income.

Lock the Doors

Security is a must in the digital world. Just like in the physical world, locks only keep out the honest and the lazy. Even so, it's important to be diligent and do what you can to keep your information and any customer information you have safe.

Basic security applies not only to your website, but all of your digital presence:

- Keep your computer safe, and use antivirus, malware, and firewall tools.
- Passwords
  - Use strong passwords. Never use your name, email address or other personal identification in the password such as birthdays, anniversaries or pet names.
  - Do not share your password across multiple sites or accounts.
  - Change passwords frequently, every 90 days or if you have reason to believe it's been compromised.
  - Do not share your password with someone you do not trust. Reputable companies and service providers will never ask you for a username, password or account information over the phone.
- If you receive an email from a service provider, do not click through the links. Log into their website separately from the email.
- Question everything, especially if it feels odd. Microsoft will not call you about a problem with your laptop. Your ISP will not ask you for your name and password.

When you use services for your website hosting, cloud storage (Google Drive, iCloud, Dropbox, etc.), email lists (MailChimp, MadMimi, MailerLite, etc.), payment processing (banks, Square, Stripe, etc.) these give you a level of security for your customers they store the information, not you. In many of these cases, their protection goes both ways. By using these services as part of your internet presence, and selling through reputable services, your readers and customers will feel safer doing business with you.

Use security certificates with your site. When you see https:// versus http://, that means the traffic between your customer and your website is encrypted and more secure. This is done as part of your configuration process. Google Chrome and other browsers and internet security tools will flag sites with scary warning pages when they do not use security certificates.

Minimize the amount of information you capture or store about customers. If you have an authenticated area (where they can log into or leave comments) you will need to keep them secure. Even if you don't capture personal information such as phone numbers and legal address, you want to make sure your site is secure, and no "bad actors" (and I don't mean B-movie stars) can hijack your site for their own purposes, because they can.

- Use a reputable hosting service.
- Keep your site up to date. WordPress and other platforms can do this for you automatically.
- Check your site on a regular basis, watch for abnormal traffic.
- Use Google Analytics (it's free) to track activity on your site.
- Back your site up any time you make a change.
- Use reputable themes, plugins and add-ons.
- Use security, antivirus and firewall plugins and services on your website.

There are a lot of tech type changes you can make, all of which can improve the performance and security of your website, but address the most important at least.

Have You Got the Look?

We have talked about what needs to be on your website from a content standpoint, but it is also critical to remember your website represents you, your brand, and your products. When people visit your site, they are looking to get more information about you, but like all people, the real question your visitors ask is, *what's in it for me?*

For people to come spend time with you and your site, much less return, there has to be value and benefit to them.

Here are some considerations that feed into your customer's user experience:

- Does your site immediately reflect you, your work, your art, and your services? Can I tell you are a writer, and what you write about? That you are an editor? An artist? If you write political thrillers, do you have the capitol dome exploding, or a penguin tap dancing?

- Is the tone of your blog, your bio, and anything else reflective of you and the brand you want to present? Does your voice and style come through? Did you run spell check? You are the editor here.

- Is the visual design clean and consistent? Use colors that call people to action boldly and consistently. Images should reflect you and your brand. Embrace the user experience.

- Does the reader get benefit from visiting daily? Weekly? Every three years?

- Once they are there, does the reader know what to do? Where to go? Is there a clear call to action to buy your wares or sign up for your newsletter?

- Does your site appear professional and credible as a place to do business?

In addition to all of the pages and elements previously described, you should also have fun with your site. There are a lot of ways to create a "Value Added" experience for your visitors. Remember, they are your guests, not family, when they visit your site. You should update it regularly. If something is out of date, get rid of it. Always be looking for ways to improve your public persona and presence.

I've Got a Blog, and Nothing to Say

Now you have a blog. So what? The blank page stares back at you. Who is going to read this anyway? What do the hypothetical "they" even want to see?

It depends. Who are you, and what do you want to accomplish through your blog?

- If you are working as an expert or a specialist in your field, share insights from your work that people in your field will find valuable or interesting. Share experiences from your career. If you are a chef, share a few recipes or a video. If you work in technology, share the latest hints and innovations that interest you. Fiction writers can bring in topics related to their latest book, or work in progress.
- Offer something for stopping by. A special short story for signing up for your mailing list. Pages with character biographies or diary entries from what they are up to between books.
- Pictures you used for inspiration and reference in writing the story.
- Share and highlight the work of others (with proper attributions of course).
- Share fan experiences and letters (with names redacted of course).
- Talk about what you are watching, reading, or listening to for inspiration.
- Share a little about your current research or project.
- Audio and video files from your speaking engagements and media events. If you have a YouTube channel, or the creator of the media has the video, add links or embed it in your site. If you were on TV or radio, show it off! It's your time to shine.
- Offer incentives, giveaways, or even just interactive activities such as "ask the author."
- Include cut scenes from books, like extras on the DVD, or sneak peeks into what is coming next.

In short, your blog posts can be about anything. You can be personal with what you write, but please do not overshare. Be professional (see a theme yet?). Even if you are not yet published, this gives you a baseline to work from and helps you develop a following before your work is ready and available. It can even help you close that first deal with an agent or publisher by having an established presence.

I've Done all That. Now what?

You have completed your first blog post. Or tenth. Or hundredth. In one of those "do as I say, not as I do" moments, post to your blog regularly. Feed it, nurture it, and watch your audience grow. A little sunlight helps as well.

It is unlikely your website and your blog will have a hundred hits the first day. Or maybe even one. It is much like building an audience for your books. You have to work to get noticed. Depending on how and why you use the blog and your website, you may only be pursuing a small or niche audience. Or you may be looking for throngs of millions.

There are almost as many ways to generate traffic and give people reasons to visit you as there are people in your audience. You just need to let them know you exist first.

Here are ways to generate exposure and traffic for your website:

- Guest posts and guest blogging with others in your field or in your areas of interest builds relationships with others in your niche. You can often exchange posts and create backlinks with those sites which helps your traffic and SEO rankings, and those of the other site.

- Build a network of people with whom you share each other's posts via social media. Cross post when you're at events together. You may even all share posts in a common or shared site, and cross share each other's posts on your own blogs.

- WordPress and other engines feature "Reblogging" which lets you repost other people's posts (with citations and references back to the original source) on your own site. While I would not suggest doing it all the time, if you share things you find interesting, others will as well.

- Posting updates and blog posts via social media will draw additional interest and traffic. WordPress can do this for you automatically.

- Keep posting high quality material people will be interested in.

- Link your blog through social bookmarking sites, such as Pinterest, SlashDot, or Reddit. Some of them are specialized, others are general sites that let you link and index your blog for users to find.

- Pinging websites such as Ping-O-Matic and Pingoat are services that force search engines such as Google to refresh their view of your website.

- Use Really Simple Syndication (RSS, sometimes called Rich Site Summary) so people can subscribe to your blog and automatically receive updates in their browsers, podcast aggregators or in system generated emails. If you use WordPress, there is native technology to help you build the feeds and plugins can make it easier.

- Let your mailing list know every time you have a blog update, or a regular summary as a part of your email updates.

- Within your blog posts and website pages you can also use SEO to increase traffic and visibility of your posts as well:
  - Use tagging and keywords in your posts so search engines will find specific articles and bring people to you.

o Create links inside of blog posts to other posts of yours or others. If the post is part of a series, link them together.

o Write compelling headlines that go with great posts. I recommend every writer study copyrighting to tighten your writing, create better blurbs for your books, and have more compelling advertising. Check out Ann Handley's Everybody Writes and The Copywriter's Handbook by Robert W. Bly for starters.

At the end of the day, putting out quality product and connecting with people brings success. While you may get lucky and have something go viral, building and keeping an audience is a long-term game.

Getting Noticed

The biggest hurdle most authors face is obscurity. Marketing, advertising, personal appearances and social media are all things we spend time and money on to raise our brand awareness.

In the digital world, we use search engines (Google, Bing, Yahoo, etc.) to find information, whether it is movie times, the life cycle of the mosquito, or how to make a living from writing. These tools search (crawl) through public websites, pages, and information to build a profile of what's in them. Ranking algorithms (a formula that parses the information to see what the most relevant information from your request) are displayed. eCommerce sites such as Amazon do the same thing when you are looking for a book or product based on your search terms.

Why is this important to you? If you are creating names for your projects, writing blog posts or posting to social media, you want them to be found. This is a process called SEO or Search Engine Optimization. If you are making the effort to be active, understanding the basics of SEO will reward your efforts.

There is no optimal combination of hints for SEO. And if there were, by next Tuesday it would be out of step. Instead, we will talk about what can help and hurt you from an SEO standpoint:

- "Content is king" is an old adage, and it is one of the biggest factors in SEO. Based on the algorithms that scan and index publicly available information, the more and better content you have on your site, the better your rankings. Most people using search engines never go past the first page of results.

- When you write the title for an article or post, make it pop. Use powerful language over generic. "Award-winning Titles at Bottom Shelf Prices" over "Thousands of books, cheap!"

- Boost the potency of your writing by understanding the keywords relevant to your material. There are a number of services and sites that can help you identify keywords and phrases that will boost your rankings. Monitor keywords for your subject and topic, since they change over time.

- When considering keywords, consider how you name your permalinks (the permanent address for a web page or blog post) and the names of pictures or other media on your site. Those also are highly weighted by SEO algorithms. Https://www.yourwebsite.here/How-To-Self-Edit is more friendly, useful and will draw a lot more traffic than the obliquely named https://www.yourwebsite.here/blogpost101.

- Having a site map linking to all of your major pages and areas improves navigation for both users and the tools that crawl a site.

- Links with other sites and content is a big boost. If you post to another site, link the article back to you (such as contributing to a news site, and linking back to your own website and social media accounts). It also makes it easier for potential fans to find you. Much like in the real world, connections and relationships with others raises your visibility and credibility (depending on your connections.)

- Backlinks are links within your own site that reference prior articles, and create a web of information within your site. For example, if you write a three-part article, link each to the other so that the reader and the search engine can easily create connections. Also, if you have mentioned a key idea or concept as a part of your expertise, linking to prior articles helps in the same way.

- Pinging can help boost you as well. This tells the search engines you have updated your website and want them to crawl it. Examples include http://pingler.com/ and http://pingomatic.com/. Pinging is more effective when you have large content updates or have new backlinks on your site or linked to others. Pinging too often or when there are no changes can hurt you as they appear less reputable or "spammy."

- Keep your technologies updated. Use the current versions of your website platforms as much as is possible. Also, eliminating outdated technologies, such as Flash, helps. The speed and performance of your site weighs heavily on SEO. For example, if you have a WordPress site, turn on automatic updates. If you do, make sure to test the site regularly to ensure an update doesn't break anything. I recommend building a regression test plan.

- Not only are social media platforms designed for marketing, it's the lifeblood of search engines. Paid advertising gets you to the top of search results in what is known as Search Engine Advertising (SEA). If you are running ads on Google for example, make sure you are using keywords and content that match to what you promise to deliver.

For any one of these topics, there are hundreds of books, articles and videos talking about how to improve. There is not a silver bullet that will rocket you to the top, but it is easy to knock yourself down. Search engines are designed to return the best results from a query and hide risky or sub-par results. They aren't there for your benefit, but for the searcher.

And a word of warning, there are a lot of legitimate ways to boost your SEO ranking, but there are just as many ways to hurt yourself as well. Whether you or someone else builds and maintains your website, make sure to stay to the white hat rules of SEO and SEA.

Monetization

Your website and other owned media offer a number of ways to generate additional revenues. A few common examples are:

- Amazon, Google AdWords, and other eCommerce businesses have affiliate programs. With these programs, you allow those companies to advertise on your blog, in your newsletters, and other places through digital media. There are different models. You receive either a flat fee or a percentage of the sales for a period of time from that site (based on clicks and products purchased).
- YouTube and other social media sites will share a small portion of advertising revenues based on your number of subscribers/followers, and on the number of ads that are clicked through or viewed.
- Direct sale of or exchange of space for advertising on your website, podcast, and other digital media activity.

Don't Feed the Trolls

"In order for me to be hurt by you, I have to respect you. I don't respect these hateful Internet trolls who have nothing better to do than attack my looks or the way I speak."
- Tomi Lahren

In Scandinavian folklore, the troll is a hideous creature, more beast than man, living in the remote wilderness. We're all familiar with children's stories of the troll under the bridge, waiting for the hapless traveler.

The modern internet troll can be much worse (often shown as the forty-year-old gamer still living in their mother's basement), lying in wait to pounce on the happy-go-lucky digital surfer (like a hot pocket newly freed from the microwave) to make an innocent but stupid comment. While the troll of myth lived cursed, but on instinct, their digital counterparts come from a place of fear and self-loathing, wishing everyone else the same misery.

So, would it surprise you, that's not the origin of the use in reference to these sad creatures?

It comes from fishing. Yep, fishing. If you have ever gone deep sea fishing, or watched the Discovery Channel, you see the fishing boats haul nets, or drop-baited fishing lines into the water. This is called trawling or trolling. The boat slowly cuts a swath through the ocean, picking up fish along the way. Sometimes they even reel in the big haul.

According to the Oxford English Dictionary, the term "troll" was first used December 14, 1992 in a Usenet group. For those who don't remember those days, this was the period of moving away from bulletin board systems (BBS') and into the early web pages of the world wide web. Triggering "flame wars" was a sport among the hardest of hard-core geeks and nerds. I hate to admit, they could be fun to watch. Sometimes, you barely had to bait the hook.

Since that time social media, the proliferation of websites, and eCommerce has opened up all sorts of behavior ranging from sarcastic comments to verbal assaults, stalking and bullying. The media latched onto the term "internet troll" and "trolling" for any behavior deemed antisocial or inappropriate. While laws are catching up to deal with criminal offenders, it's no longer (and never was) just lonely geeks. Perceived anonymity and mob mentality both lead to inappropriate behavior that most of these people would never do in person.

As an author and business owner, expect that not everyone is going to love and worship you. A lot of them aren't even going to like you or your work. They aren't your customer, and they aren't your tribe. It doesn't matter, and doesn't deserve any of your energy or attention. Even top best-selling authors get bad reviews.

The important lesson is this: there will always be people who thrive on destroying others to justify their existence and make themselves feel better. It is easy to sit behind the anonymity of the keyboard and attack others. As hard as it can be, don't engage. The moment you respond, you have lost, and they have what they wanted. They got attention, wasted your time, and feasted on your ire like the parasite they are.

Yes, there are those who want to legitimately discuss and critique your work. They are not trolls. The troll throws out a lot of lines and waits to see who bites. Once you're on the hook, if you manage to get off, it's going to hurt. There is no reasoning with the troll. No use of rationality will change their opinion.

Do not feed the troll.

Repeat: Do. Not. Feed. The. Troll.

They never get full. They never get tired.

Do not feed the troll.

Don't make justifications.

Don't make excuses.

Just do not feed the troll. Period.

Don't make me come over there.

5: Finance and Accounting

Business Plans and Financial Models

"Invest in yourself. Your career is the engine of your wealth." - Paul Clitheroe

At the core of any business is the desire to make money. One of the hardest lessons for any business owner is the fundamentals about money.

Most of us are used to the idea of going to work and getting some form of regular paycheck. It is an exchange of time and skills for money in the service of someone else's business. If you own or have interest in a business, you make your money from the business' earnings, net the expenses it costs to operate and market. No hourly rates, and no guarantees.

As an author, you are either a partner or the sole owner of the business.

Despite the fact that we enter into business to make money, finance and accounting are often the most neglected parts of the business, and what people hate to deal with the most. I've got a background in accounting; and even I hate doing the bookkeeping, so don't feel bad. With a little success, you pay someone to keep the books, and you keep cranking them out.

Successful business owners recognize money for what it is: a tool, and a measure. We have to put resources into starting a business, much like fueling ourselves to pedal the bike we have been building. If we oil and maintain the gears, keep the tires inflated, and keep ourselves fueled, the bike can take us almost anywhere. The same is true with the business, and the byproduct of success is profits.

In this section we will explore the fundamental concepts of money in business. Like the chains and gears of your bicycle, you can see them and know they are there, but it can be hard to tell how well they work, and what benefit small changes could bring.

As you learn the mechanics of how money and business fundamentals work, you will discover how to generate more revenue, and how to hold onto more of it.

For any business, there are a few pieces that build out a complete financial model:

- Financial statements tell you the health of your business, where your money comes from, and where it goes.
- Budgets detail financial goals balanced against financial statements and tell you how well you are doing against your plan (plan versus actual).
- Business plans take not only your financial plan, but all of the pieces of your business and pulls it into one place. (This book is largely designed around the functions of a business, and how to plan for each.)

Revenues (Got to Get Paid!)

"Remind people that profit is the difference between revenue and expense. This makes you look smart."
- Scott Adams

At the end of every business is the (hopefully) big reward. While adoration and recognition are nice, they don't pay the bills. We are all looking for the pot of gold at the end of the Amazon rainbow.

As a writer, you have to find the income streams that best suit you. Refer back to the sections on **The People of the Business** and **Up the Revenue Stream Without a Paddle**, where we explored the most common roles and types of work in publishing and utilizing content to get the most from it. Having multiple sources of income takes away some of the risk if something fails, and levels out your income.

But it's time to discuss one of the more misunderstood parts of business. Revenues vs. a paycheck.

With few exceptions, everyone reading this book is going to have received a paycheck from an employer. The first time you ever saw a paycheck, you were probably a little surprised to see the gross amount vs. the net after all of the taxes and deductions. Maybe, you still are.

As a small business owner, you don't receive a paycheck. With any luck, you'll be able to make a profit, and pay yourself. For businesses, money coming in the door are called revenues.

So why is this important?

A paycheck is you trading your skills and time to someone else in exchange for money.

Revenues are monies coming into your business in an exchange for your time, expertise, products and services. (And remember, it's never a sin to be paid for the fruits of your labor, knowledge, skills, expertise, and unique view of the world.)

So, what's the real difference?

Once you receive the paycheck, it's yours to use as you want and need. Revenues, on the other hand, are the life blood of your business which you use to pay the expenses related to your operations and fund the growth of your business. And once all of that is done, you pay yourself from what is left over.

Revenues for people in the publishing world come from a number of different products and services, determined by your products and business model. These are called revenue streams. As an entrepreneur and business owner you need to consider any and all sources of revenue that fit your brand, products, and your skill set. Sometimes, it can even make sense to set up different revenue streams under different businesses.

Some examples of sources of revenue streams are:

- Book sales – be they through retailers, book (magazine, newspaper, etc.) sales are the life blood of the author.
- Advances - If you sell your work to a traditional publisher, you may receive an advance before or after the piece is written. If you are contracted to do a specific work, the publisher may give you an advance based on expected sales. Direct expenses factor into the advance. Be aware of the idea of earning out your advance, which is the point book sales exceed advanced royalties, and you have earned additional compensation from future book sales. Remember, an advance on royalties is just that: an advance.
- Royalties - The commissions paid for sales of books through your publisher or other direct seller on your behalf. Royalties are paid as a percentage of the cover price or sale price.
- Residuals - The royalties paid after your book has "earned out" or sold more than the percentage due paid on advances.
- Direct sales - Sales of books by the author to others at signings, events, etc. This comes from inventory provided to you by your publisher either for free by contract, or which you have purchased at a discounted rate.
- Speaking/appearance fees - If you have expertise in some subject(s), or the ability to entertain, you can be paid for appearances at events and conventions. Having a book (or books) can be the driver for getting these types of appearances, or additional revenue if your primary business model is personal appearances.
- Editing - As a service, many writers also provide editing services for other writers.
- Marketing - Consulting and advising on building markets, and cross promotion.
- Other services - Experience and expertise has value, and there are services such as ghost writing, story development, personal assistants etc.
- Affiliate links and advertising on your website.

Each of these revenue streams has their own unique investments and expenses as well as the ability to create revenue. Find what works for you, and your business.

How Does Money Work in Publishing?

We have touched on money numerous times, but now we will distill it down to the key concepts. Understanding revenues for authors can be like Schrodinger's cat; you don't know what's going on in the box until it's time to open it, and you can't be sure what will come out the other end until you do.

Traditional publishing, be it through one of the big New York houses or a small publisher have the same fundamental mechanics:

- Money flows towards the author, and the author is not responsible for any of the costs related to the production of the book (Yog's law). The exception is self-publishing (below).
- If you have an agent, the money flows through the agency and the agent gets their cut first. The agent passes the balance to the author(s). Agents only get paid when you do.
- Authors are paid "royalties," which is a form of licensing the intellectual property of one or more people, and then paying them a share of the revenues. Royalties will often be calculated as a percentage of the sales price, or the gross revenues.
- A publisher may pay an advance on royalties, often shortened to calling it an "advance." This is, in essence, a loan the publisher is giving the author with an expectation of the number of copies the book will sell. Advances are usually paid in three installments: when the contract is signed, when the final draft is received and accepted by the publisher, and when the book is released. If a book does not earn out, typically the remaining balance of the advance does not have to be repaid, but if the book is not delivered or meet contractual standards, some portion may be payable back to the publisher.
- If the publisher pays an advance, the author will receive no additional monies until the book has "earned out," or has earned enough royalties to cover what has been paid in the advance.

Self-publishing puts all of the risk and rewards directly on the author. Yog's law does not apply.

- The author is both the author and publisher and is responsible for all investments and decisions.
- Royalties paid by Amazon and other distributors are not true royalties. They are sales commissions and are taxed like regular income. Royalties paid by publishers are taxed differently.
- The royalties paid for print books are determined by the price of the book less the cost, and a factor to determine the final commission payable to the author.

- Ebook royalties differ by vendor and program. For example, going deep (exclusive) with Amazon means the author is eligible for their maximum royalty rates (70% at the time of this writing) while going wide (multiple distributors) caps royalties at 35%.
- Kindle Unlimited royalties are paid from a pool of shares based on page reads.
- Audiobook royalties are determined by the distributor. If you use ACX, royalties are determined by if you directly paid the narrator and producer or if you used a royalty split. Whether the audiobook was purchased or bought as a member of Audible's plans all affect the pricing and royalty paid.

This only begins to explain the high points of royalties for authors, and once you start receiving royalty statements, you will find additional complexities. And as a rule of thumb, if you think you are owed money, ask. Especially if your agent just bought a new beach house in Costa Rica, and you haven't seen a royalty check in six months.

For more information, money in publishing is one of the modules included in John Hartness' "Path to Publication" workshop, available through **https://www.authoressentialsworkshops.com/**.

Operating Capital

Moving forward with your business, the next key is how to get the resources you need. Depending on the particulars of your business, you'll need specific assets (money, laptops, software, etc.). No matter what you're doing, you'll always need operating capital.

Operating capital is the financing, cash, and available credit to keep your business going and growing. Let's assume for a moment you're still in the startup phase. You may or may not have your first project complete and are looking to move forward. During this time, in most scenarios, you will be funding most, if not all of the work out of your own pocket. In rare circumstances, an unknown and unpublished author may be given an advance for their story before it's developed, but this is rare, and typically involves an experienced co-author.

In both the **Business Plans** and the **Operational Budgets** sections, you'll see planning become critical as you fund your project, and the business overhead. Budgets tell you how much you need to raise, and help you balance the expected return.

Different types and sources of funding/revenues:

- *Your own capital*: You're often the one fronting and maintaining the capital and cash flow required, especially in the early stages. Take your business and project expenses into account with your personal budget and cash flow.
- *Book advance*: If you are contracted to develop a book, an advance on royalties helps cover your expenses, and part of your eventual returns. Keep in mind, if the project falls apart or you fail to deliver, you may be liable for part, or all, of the advance to the publisher.
- *Crowdfunding*: Additional details are in the section on crowdfunding, but remember, this is a difficult challenge, especially for an unknown author.
- *Sponsored/contract work*: Contracted writing both hones skills and provides cash flow with the added benefit of publishing credits. This can include contributing to online news sources, blogs, websites, copy writing, and creating commercial content.
- *Advertising*: Running ads on your website can help defray costs and generate positive revenue.
- *Affiliate programs*: A specific type of advertising where you can earn residuals not only from your products, but other products and services bought after site visitors click through from your website. Amazon, Google, and other online sellers have affiliate programs.

As with all businesses, you need to manage both revenues and cash flow, and find revenues that match your business.

Operating Expenses

As with any business, you have to invest to get returns, and there's the cost of doing business. Not only will you need to pay expenses but track them for a tax basis. (Hint, you may be able to deduct expenses as a business owner you couldn't as an employee.)

There are several types of expenses you can expect:
- Fixed - expenses that happen on a regular basis and at a known rate. For example, this would be your mortgage, or rent on your office space. It also would be certain utilities such as phone or internet.
- Variable - expenses that happen on a regular basis but change in amount.
  o Utilities - water and electric
  o Supplies - office supplies, coffee, etc.
  o Taxes

- Periodic - Expenses that are driven by a specific project, activity, or may regularly occur over a long period.
  o Website fees (these are often charged annually).
  o Marketing for a book launch.
  o Travel expenses related to research or appearances.
  o Dues for organizations or societies.
  o Subscriptions, such as periodicals or websites that provide research sources, journals on writing as a business, etc.
  o Subscriptions to digital services, such as Microsoft, Adobe, and other "software as a service" products (Software as a Service, SaaS).
  o Books and other research or professional development materials.
  o Convention booth expenses.
  o A new laptop, printer, etc.

As the owner of the business, you're responsible for everything. That means, most of all, funding your business and your projects. There are two big components: how much do you need, and where will the funds come from?

Learning to understand and anticipate your expenses will allow you to better manage them, and the cash flow required. The better you track them from an accounting standpoint will help you manage your tax bill and gain information to project for future budgets.

Cost of Goods Sold (COGS)

In the business world, it makes sense to understand how much a product costs to determine if you are making a profit or not. Costs are classified as either direct or indirect expenses.

Knowing how much each book costs you helps you to price the book and determine how many need to be sold to turn a profit.

Direct expenses are those specifically tied to the cost of developing, producing and bringing your products to market.

If you are working through a traditional publisher, you are not responsible for the production costs of developing or producing the book. (Money flows towards the author.) Examples would be:

- Editing the book for publication, including developmental if required.
- Covers and graphic artwork for your book.
- Agent commissions are tied directly to sales. They get paid when you do.

Some other expenses may be reimbursed, depending on the terms of your contract, such as:

- Travel or research related costs to developing the book.
- Materials or licenses purchased related to the content, such as images included inside the book.
- Editing contracted outside of the services directly provided by the publisher.

If you are self-publishing, or acting as the publisher, you are responsible for all of the costs and expenses related to development and production:

- Editing Expenses.
- Cover Art.
- Licensing of pictures and other art used inside the book or for promotion.
- Formatting and preparation for release.
- Production of the audiobooks.

Print costs - The features that will weigh heavily on the cost to print, and factor into retail pricing.

- Bindings are commonly glued, but there are different grades and qualities of bindings. Hardback books tend to have the greatest options and variance in bindings.
- Covers for hardbacks can vary in materials. Niche books may be leather-bound or in specialty materials with filigree. You may also have printed dust covers. Paperbacks can feature different qualities in material.
- Page count will be a determining factor in the overall cost of the book, and is affected by the dimensions of the book (trade paperback, digest, novel, textbook, etc.), the font and size, and the margins.
- Page material can also vary from low bond to linen and almost any material in between. Most print solutions will provide several options.
- Artwork and images, both in terms of cover art and images inside the book can increase printing costs depending on color versus grayscale.
- Interior color increases printing costs significantly. If you are producing a book with a large number of color images, the paper stock used and overall printing costs for those pages are significantly higher. With the management and printing of high quality images, differences in paper stock and additional effort is a factor as well.

- Shipping costs also have to be considered as a part of the per-unit cost.

Indirect expenses or "overhead" are those related to the overall operation of your business, and not necessarily tied to one product or campaign:
- Your website and other owned media expenses.
- Marketing and advertising costs.
- Publicists.
- Sales commissions (can be direct or indirect).
- Trade show/event costs.
- Office equipment.
- Software licenses.
- Organizational dues.
- Assistants or other operational costs.

Calculating your Cost of Goods Sold is done by taking all of the direct costs for the product + an overhead factor (indirect expense). As you allocate indirect expenses, you have to calculate a share of your total overhead to each sale. When budgeting, you can do this by estimating how many of each product you will sell in a given year and divide that across the products.

As you will see in the example below, each version of a product can have its own cost and overhead version:

Sample COGS

Product		Book 1	Ebook 1	Audiobook 1	Ebook 2	Total
Estimated Sales (count)		1,000	10,000	7,500	5,000	
Gross Sale Price		19.95	4.99	49.95	4.99	
Estimated Revenues		19,950	49,900	374,625	24,950	469,425
Direct Costs (per unit)						
Commission		9.98	1.50	24.98	1.50	
Revenue Share				12.49		
Printing		6.10				
Shipping		0.97				
Total Direct Costs/unit		17.05	1.50	37.46	1.50	
Gross Margin/unit		*2.91*	*3.49*	*12.49*	*3.49*	
Gross Margin		*2,905.00*	*34,930.00*	*93,662.49*	*17,465.00*	*148,962.49*
Overhead calculation						
Product Specific Costs						
Editing		0.36	0.36		0.60	
Cover		0.05	0.05	0.04	0.10	
General Overhead	Allocation	1.95%	23.45%	62.88%	11.72%	
Website	4,000	0.08	0.09	0.34	0.09	
Marketing	10,000	0.20	0.23	0.84	0.23	
Total Overhead/unit		*0.68*	*0.74*	*1.21*	*1.03*	
Total Overhead		*682.11*	*7,373.75*	*9,102.72*	*5,141.42*	*22,300.00*
Net Income/unit		*2.22*	*2.76*	*11.27*	*2.46*	
Estinated Net Income		*2,222.89*	*27,556.25*	*84,559.78*	*12,323.58*	*126,662.49*

The assumptions used are:

- The costs of editing ($4,000) and the covers ($500) is split across the print and ebooks over 11,000 estimated copies.
- The audiobook cover was a separate charge ($300) over 7,500 copies. The assumption is a revenue share model (50/50 split) for the recording and production of the audiobook.
- The editing ($3,000) and cover ($500) of book 2 were allocated over 5,000 copies.
- Digital product commissions are based on Amazon rates, and print copies on bookstore commissions.
- The general overhead was split taking the gross expense and creating a ratio of the projected revenues as a percentage of the whole and multiplying that against the estimated number of books sold. (Ex. Book 1, print = (2,905/133,992.49) * $4,000 = $.09 per book allocation for the website expense.)

Using these factors, you can also put a value on your inventory, if you have any.

Pricing

You have invested time and resources to develop and bring your work to market. If you are going through a traditional publisher or distributor, they will typically set the cover prices.

If you are the publisher for a product, or are self-publishing, figuring out how much to charge for your products and services can be a challenge. Will you do promotional pricing? Do you need a loss leader? Can you bundle products to create and incentivize the deal?

All of this and more feeds into your pricing strategies.

Some guidelines to use if you are either the publisher or are self-publishing:

- Hardback/paperback books - your distributor, typically a print-on-demand service (KDP Select (formerly CreateSpace), Lulu, etc.) will give you the cost of printing the book and shipping. Good rule of thumb is to value it based on what it will cost to place on consignment in an independent bookstore. On average, the author/publisher should split 20% of the cover price. This can be calculated by taking the cost to print and ship the book and multiply that by 60%, then double it. For an average $20 book, the bookstore will take 50% of the cover price ($10). It costs $6 to print and ship, leaving $4 to be split between the author and publisher. If you are self-publishing, you get 20% in this model.

- Ebooks - as Amazon is the largest distributor on the planet, they tend to set the standards. As of the time of this writing (and has been for years) Amazon has a strategy where ebooks should be ideally priced between $2.99 and $9.99. They manage this by controlling the "royalties" percentage paid per book to incentivize the author. They also have incentives for exclusive distribution through Amazon.
- Audiobooks - As Audible (by Amazon) is a major distributor, and ACX their production arm, the price of the audiobook is set by the length of the audio. The creator has no control over the pricing. Also, different prices and royalties are paid if the customer is an Audible member, and if the monthly credits are used or if the book is purchased directly.

Taxes

There's an old saying. There are only two certainties, but when it comes to small business the second one is a pressing concern. Taxes.

Most of us are accustomed to seeing large chunks of cash disappear to "withholding" in our paychecks and the sales taxes we pay when we go shopping. Now that you are a business, you get to find out about the other side of taxes. I handle it here as a liability and not an expense because it is accrued and due to be paid on a regular periodic basis. It's a liability until it is actually paid.

Where you live, how, and where your business operates, will determine the taxes for which you are liable. If you're not certain, please consult with your Department of Revenue and/or a tax accountant. This list is not exhaustive, but does address the more common ones:

- Income taxes are paid based on a percentage of your net income, or your revenues less allowable expenses. Not all expenses are deductible. Here are the most common income taxes you may encounter in the United States. Other countries have similar structures:
  - o Individual income taxes, for unincorporated businesses, all of your business revenues and expenses will flow through your individual income taxes and contribute to your Adjusted Gross Income (AGI). If you are incorporated, distributions will be taxed for you individually. Distributions can be made in the form of a salary, bonuses, distributive shares, draws, dividends or some combination depending on the type of business. Most authors will take it in the form of a draw unless you have formed an S-corp when you will take distributive shares. This determines how the income is taxed.
  - o Corporate income taxes apply if you have incorporated your business. You may have to file corporate income taxes depending on the style of incorporation. (S-Corps flow through your regular individual return.)
  - o Self-employment taxes are calculated based on the net income of your business. In your typical withholding, you are accountable for half of your Medicare Insurance and Social Security taxes, and your employer the other half. In this case, you are your own employer, and will be liable for the entire allocation.
- State income taxes are calculated based on a percentage of your federal Adjusted Gross Income.

- City/municipality income taxes are calculated based on a percentage of your Federal Adjusted Gross Income.
- Sales Taxes are assessed depending on where the sales are made, and others depending on the location of your business. Many authors sell books at conventions and events and may do so across multiple states and localities. You will be responsible for being aware of and paying any state and local sales or use taxes. At the time of this writing, if you do internet sales through your own website, under certain volumes you may not be accountable for sales tax, but this may be changing. Outside of the United States, various forms of sales or VAT (Value Added Taxes) taxes are common.
- Business Licenses - Depending on your business structure, you may be required to have a business license based on your state and local laws.

Assets and Liabilities

"Most people... find a disorientating mismatch between the long-term nature of their liabilities and the increasingly short-term nature of their assets."
- James A. Baldwin

There is a stark truth hidden in this statement. Most assets depreciate over time or have some risk attached to them. Liabilities hold a certain unchanging truth. I will balance this against another statement,

Assets put money in your pocket, whether you work or not, and liabilities take money from your pocket.
- Robert Kiyosaki

When you look at your balance sheet, the formula is:

$$assets - liabilities = owner's\ equity.$$

Another way of stating the owner's equity is net worth. Are you worth more than you owe?

It's easy to get bogged down in the numbers sometimes or even feel that sinking feeling when you look at a credit card statement after a couple of weeks of conventions.

I draw from both of these quotes as they help define the way you should look at the assets and liabilities that make up your business. As you look at the figures, you need to ask yourself if the asset is bringing value and benefit to your business and if the liabilities have helped you acquire something of value.

For any business, resources are limited and need to be utilized as efficiently as possible. There are several types of resources to consider:

- Liquid and credit (capital) resources to finance business activities includes cash, investments, and debt instruments (loans, mortgages, bonds). These may take the form of assets or liabilities, or asset backed liabilities,
- Tangible and intangible assets include physical assets as well as intellectual property brought into, utilized, expended and created by the business.
- Human resources and capital are the most critical in creative enterprises. This includes your time and skills, those of your partners, and anyone you might bring in for specific services.

Over time, we all learn that some things that appear to hold value are not assets, and that spending resources to gain something of value is not a liability. Focus on making the most of what you have, identifying what you need, and what may be an albatross around your neck.

Assets

Assets are resources you bring into the business or acquire, including tangible and intangible. Depending on the business structure, assets can be handled in multiple ways.

When bringing personal assets into a business or purchasing assets for a business, ensure you have agreements about the ownership of those assets if you have partners in the event the business relationship is dissolved.

- Tangible or physical assets have a relatively fixed physical value, and most will depreciate over time. This includes your car, computers, office equipment, and inventory if you use it as a part of the business. Depreciation is a reduction in the value of a tangible asset because of use, age, and maintenance. For tax purposes, it is calculated based on the asset's "useful life." A fully depreciated asset does not mean it cannot be used or has no value, but it carries none for accounting purposes.

    As an author, real property could become an asset of the business, or providing leverage for the business. For example, you may take out a mortgage or use home equity lines of credit to support the needs of your business and career.

- Intangible assets are the ones you bring into the business including your brand and your name. In writing and publishing, you are creating the valuable intangible asset of intellectual property. While you may think of the physical book as an asset you can sell, intangibles are the ideas, copyrights, brands, websites, and other non-physical products of your work.

For purposes of this book, we are assuming you are producing intangible assets in the form of protected intellectual property.

Risks and Liabilities

Liabilities are a factor of business and economic systems. They arise any time you have a real or potential debt.

Taking on debt is not a bad thing in itself. To grow a company takes resources. To decide if you even want to attempt entering a business means research and sometimes investing in educating yourself. It also means taking risks. It doesn't mean taking uninformed risks. Not every good opportunity is the right opportunity. Early on, you have to say yes to try ideas out and build your reputation. Later on, you have to say no to what is only a good opportunity and but a great one for you.

Financial liabilities come in three classifications:
- Short-term (current) liabilities are due to be paid within one year, such as revolving credit (credit cards), tax liabilities, utilities and accounts payable for product.
- Long-term (non-current) liabilities are due and payable in installments or a balloon covering more than one year, such as mortgages and leases.
- Contingent liabilities are created based on conditional events. Lawsuits, insurance claims, and warranties fall into this category.

While none of us like to be in debt, few businesses can start without encountering some. It is almost always a factor in buying a house or car, and credit cards make online and travel much easier. The key is being deliberate about the debt you take on, and make sure it furthers your goals.
- Non-financial liabilities can bear a heavier burden. People working for you who don't fit into your team, negative people in your life, or just having the wrong assets can all create financial, brand and reputational risks.
  - Hiring or contracting someone to help you that does not understand or act in accordance with your goals can cause more work than they save, or even damage your business and reputation. Think about handing over your social media management to someone else. You are giving another person the keys to your public face. They are acting on your behalf.
  - I have had to trust my teams for all of my career, whether I built them or not. Often, it's meant building relationships and trust with people I didn't know, and even our goals and directives may have been at odds to achieve a common goal.
- An asset can be a liability in disguise. For example, buying a large house or car at the wrong time brings with it the mortgage and payments, which affect cash flow. Imagine inheriting a family hunting cabin, and taking on maintenance costs, taxes, or other forms of upkeep, or even emotional burdens. Inheriting or being given an asset that does not serve you brings risk and stress.

As a business owner, I can't repeat this often enough: you are responsible for your vision and to lead your people where you want to go. Understanding the risks and true cost of liabilities is the winding path to profit and prosperity.

Inventory

Inventory is anything you have sitting around that is ready for sale, or is a raw material to be put into a product for sale.

Inventory is calculated by:
1. Taking your existing inventory
2. Adding the cost of the product, shipping, and other direct costs.
3. Subtracting the value of product sold, lost, destroyed, or otherwise no longer available for sale.

There are four ways to value the inventory sold:
*   *Exact cost (specific identification)* is calculating the cost of the exact product at the time it was added.
*   *First-in, first-out (FIFO)* is calculated by taking the cost of the oldest inventory, and assuming that it is what was sold.
*   *Last-in, first-out (LIFO)* is calculated by taking the cost of the most recently received product and using that cost basis.
*   *Weighted average* is calculated based on taking the value of the total inventory and dividing that by the amount of product on hand to come up with an average.

For most authors, they carry such a small amount of inventory, the valuation method is irrelevant. You do need a method to use when calculating your cost of goods sold (COGS). Otherwise, it is tracking the amount of inventory on hand to know when you need to order more.

In the sample valuation, I am only using the exact cost method. Most of you should not be carrying enough inventory for the valuation method to matter. If you do, email me. Let's chat and see what I can do to help.

Sample Inventory Valuation Calculation

Order Date	Description	Number of Copies	Price	Book Cost	Shipping/Book	Total Shipping	Total Cost
January-18	Order 1	20	6.45	129.00	1.00	20.00	130.00
March-18	Order 2	25	6.75	168.75	0.85	21.25	169.60
August-18	Order 3	20	6.95	139.00	0.95	19.00	139.95
Total of Orders		**65**		**436.75**		**60.25**	**439.55**

Exact Cost							
Sale Date							
January-18	Order 1	10	6.45	64.50	1.00	10.00	65.50
April-18	Order 1	5	6.45	32.25	1.00	5.00	33.25
April-18	Order 2	12	6.75	81.00	0.85	10.20	81.85
October-18	Order 1	2	6.45	12.90	1.00	2.00	13.90
October-18	Order 2	5	6.75	33.75	0.85	4.25	34.60
October-18	Order 3	8	6.95	55.60	0.95	7.60	56.55
Total Inventory		**42**		**280.00**		**39.05**	**285.65**
Inventory Valuation		**23**		**156.75**		**21.20**	**153.90**

Exact Cost							
Sale Date							
January-18	Order 1	10	6.45	64.50	1.00	10.00	65.50
April-18	Order 1	5	6.45	32.25	1.00	5.00	33.25
April-18	Order 2	12	6.75	81.00	0.85	10.20	81.85
October-18	Order 1	2	6.45	12.90	1.00	2.00	13.90
October-18	Order 2	5	6.75	33.75	0.85	4.25	34.60
October-18	Order 3	8	6.95	55.60	0.95	7.60	56.55
Total Inventory		**42**		**280.00**		**39.05**	**285.65**
Inventory Valuation		**-19**		**(123.25)**		**(17.85)**	**(131.75)**

Exact Cost							
Sale Date							
January-18	Order 1	10	6.45	64.50	1.00	10.00	65.50
April-18	Order 1	5	6.45	32.25	1.00	5.00	33.25
April-18	Order 2	12	6.75	81.00	0.85	10.20	81.85
October-18	Order 1	2	6.45	12.90	1.00	2.00	13.90
October-18	Order 2	5	6.75	33.75	0.85	4.25	34.60
October-18	Order 3	8	6.95	55.60	0.95	7.60	56.55
Total Inventory		**42**		**280.00**		**39.05**	**285.65**
Inventory Valuation		**-61**		**(403.25)**		**(56.90)**	**(417.40)**

Exact Cost							
Sale Date							
January-18	Order 1	10	6.45	64.50	1.00	10.00	65.50
April-18	Order 1	5	6.45	32.25	1.00	5.00	33.25
April-18	Order 2	12	6.75	81.00	0.85	10.20	81.85
October-18	Order 1	2	6.45	12.90	1.00	2.00	13.90
October-18	Order 2	5	6.75	33.75	0.85	4.25	34.60
October-18	Order 3	8	6.95	55.60	0.95	7.60	56.55
Total Inventory		**42**		**280.00**		**39.05**	**285.65**
Inventory Valuation		**-103**		**(683.25)**		**(95.95)**	**(703.05)**

For accounting and tax purposes, you can recognize the cost of the books as an expense when ordered and recognize the income on sales. This is typically the simplest method, but accounting software can manage all of this for you.

Inventory has an odd characteristic. It can be both an asset and a liability at the same time.

As an author, if you want to sell a physical book at an event, you (or a vendor at the event) must have a copy in hand to sell. Assuming you want to be the one making the money, and not just taking a royalty, you will have copies on hand, an inventory.

How is my inventory an asset?

- You have a physical good to sell. You can sign it and put it in the hand of a new fan in exchange for cash.
- You have something people can see and give them a reason to see and stop to talk to you.

How could my inventory be a liability?

- You have a physical good that you have to carry with you. Books are heavy. They are bulky, especially if you are flying to the event. They are heavier when you have to take home the ones that don't sell.
- You have to buy them up front.
- They can be damaged or destroyed between engagements or conventions.
- They take up space between events.

This sounds like it could be a pain. And expensive. What can you do to find a balance between the good and bad?

First, having inventory is just a cost of doing business. Part of being an author is having a few copies around to impress people. Not to mention, it's a reminder you sat in the chair and took your words all the way to publication.

The explosion in Print on Demand (PoD) brought Just in Time (JIT) inventory for books to authors and publishers. What that means is you no longer have to order hundreds or thousands of books for a print run and manage that inventory. For traditional and self-publishing, you have the ability to order as few as one book, or as many as you need. This limits the up-front costs of the order and means you control how much of your physical space is taken up by inventory. If you have twenty titles, it can start to stack up.

We are already seeing PoD technology piloted in bookstores as well. Amazon and Barnes and Noble (as Nook Press) are both piloting programs in bookstores, airports, and other locations. This is going to open up new markets in chain bookstores for small-press-published and self-published authors.

It is up to you to determine how many copies you should keep on hand, depending on how frequently you hand sell books, but over time you will get a feel for how many you will sell at a given size event. Sometimes, you will sell your ten copies in the first hour. Other times, you may take all of them home. It's all part of learning the business, but do not order a hundred copies to sell for your first event.

The Fab Four

Year-end financial statements express a truth about office life which is no less irrefutable yet also, in the end, no less irrelevant or irritating than an evolutionary biologist's proud reminder that the purpose of existence lies in the propagation of our genes.
- Alain de Botton

Only bookkeepers and accountants really love doing financial statements. Thankfully, there are a lot of different tools you can use that will do most of the work for you, for example, Quickbooks, Quicken, Freshbooks, Netsuite, or a dozen others. I'm not making any suggestions here; they all have their pains and benefits. What is important is keeping track of the money so you know how you're doing, and so it's easier to deal with the IRS at the end of the year.

From all of the details you pull together, there are four fundamental financial statements that will be your report card:

- *Income Statements* - The Income Statement is the report that explains your profit or loss by summarizing your income (revenues) and expenses.
- *Cash Flow* - Cash Flow is the study of the ebbs and flows in the timing of your revenues and expenses. The example I present will be part of the Income Statements, though this is a separate type of financial statement in its own right.
- *Balance Sheets* - The Balance Sheet looks at the overall financial health of your company, and is made of assets, liabilities, and your equity in the company.
- *Statement of Retained Earnings* - The Equity Statement examines changes in your share of the company and your investment. For purposes of this example, it is included in the overall Balance Sheets.

Another thing many people do not consider: sometimes it makes sense to split your efforts into different businesses, each with their own financial statements. For example, you may keep your solo career as an author as a business, but if you do another project with a partner, make that its own enterprise. It will make keeping the finances straight easier and make the management part cleaner.

Numbers are a language all of their own, and learning to read them will put you ahead of ninety percent of business owners. The samples included here assume you are a new author just starting out but doing well.

Make sure you keep those receipts!

Your Income

Your Income Statement (or Profit and Loss Statement) is arguably the most important of the financial statements, because it gives you a snapshot of all of the money that came in (revenues), went out the door (expenses), and whether you made a profit or not.

If you have multiple income streams (and you should) you will want to even do a little matching, or pairing revenues with their direct expenses.

No matter what your business is, from microbusiness to the largest corporation, you need to keep track of the money coming in and going out. This is the fundamental practice of accounting.

Key Concepts:

- Revenues - Monies you've earned from your work, (or will earn if you're given an advance or retainer).
- Expenses - The expenditure of resources as part of your business activity.
- Net Income - What you have left over from your revenues after you have paid your expenses.
- Cash Basis - Recognition of a revenue or expense when cash is received, or money is spent. In other words, you record it when you get it or spend it. This will be most of you.
- Accrual Basis - Accounting for a revenue or expense before cash is exchanged. For example, if you have sold a piece of work to a publisher, you can accrue and book the receivable (what you expect to be paid) as income. You then offset accruals when money is exchanged. For example, your publisher can accrue your residuals from your book sales, and then pay you on a quarterly basis.

The basic calculation of the Income Statement is:

Your Revenues
- Cost of Goods Sold (COGS)
= Gross Margin
- Selling, General & Administrative Expenses (SG&A)
= Operating Income
+ Other Income
- Other Expenses
- Income Taxes
= Net Income or Loss

To see an easy example, we have a traditionally published author who earns most of their income from bookstore and online sales, but does a few conventions:

Sample Income Statement

		In-Person Sales	Book Royalties	eBook Royalties	AudioBook Royalties	Total
Revenues		5,000	25,000	15,000	35,000	80,000
COGS						
	Agent Commissions	750	3,750	2,250	5,250	12,000
	Books Ordered	2,500				
Total COGS		3,250	3,750	2,250	5,250	12,000
Gross Margin		1,750	21,250	12,750	29,750	68,000
SG&A Expenses						
	Owner Draw	7,000	7,000	7,000	7,000	28,000
	Hotel	1,200				1,200
	Booth Fees	450				450
	Travel	400				400
	Virtual Admin					5,000
	Marketing					15,000
	Website					4,000
Total SG&A Expenses		2,050				54,050
Operating Income		-300				13,950
Other Income						
	Loans					1,750
	Patreon					2,000
Total other income						3,750
Other Expenses						
	New laptop					2,000
	Convention wear					500
Total other expenses						2,500
Income Taxes						10,500
Net Income (Loss)						4,700

In this example, you can see the in-person sales are a loss overall but really can be treated as part of the marketing budget. I have lumped in the agent's commissions as a part of the Cost of Goods Sold, but most of the time this will be part of the Selling, General and Administrative expenses. The money you take out of the business is the "Owner Draw" (your paycheck). It's all in how you want to picture the financial health of your business.

The other important factor is to see the irregularity of cash flow, depending not only on sales but when you get paid, and having to account for periodic payments like taxes.

Your Income Statement is also a helpful tool when doing your end of year accounting, and filing your taxes, apply for loans, and any other time you have to share your income history.

The Ebb and Flow of Cash

If cash is king, cash flow is the kingdom. The success or failure of many businesses has been determined not by sales and net income but making sure the money is in the account when it is time to pay the bills. Unlike receiving a paycheck from your employer where you can typically forecast and know within reason what you will make, businesses go through ebbs and flows. As a small business, it will take time to build your business, and as a writer, cash flow is dependent on your market and sales.

Cash flow is calculated based on the cash flowing into and out of the business. It is typically compiled on a monthly basis (but you can enter and make note of it as soon as it's received or spent), but you take account of the transactions where money flows through your hands:

- Cash from operating activities - advances on royalties, royalty payments, direct sales, speaking fees, purchase of books for sale, hotel and booth costs at conventions, editing, agent fees, taxes.
- Cash from investing activities - buying or selling an asset such as a building, car or major equipment.
- Cash from financing activities - taking out loans, using credit cards, or making payments.

Cash flow can be calculated one of two ways, and is dependent on what accounting method you use:

- Direct method is used if you use the cash basis - account for revenues when they are received and liabilities when they are paid.
- The indirect method is used if you use the accrual basis - account for revenues and expenses when they are created, regardless of when cash changes hands.

I am going to assume you are using the cash basis of accounting and direct method of cash flow because it is infinitely easier and if you are generating enough income to warrant accrual, you are paying an accountant to handle it.

The digital age has redefined cash as something more than a collection of coins and bills. In fact, governments and corporations are driving a movement to the "cashless society" driven by bits and bytes. Services like PayPal, Square, and Stripe make taking electronic transactions easy and affordable for business owners, but it does come at a cost.

These tools also make it easier to track your incoming and outgoing cash flow. Many banks and some independent cloud-based services have the ability to aggregate the information for you and pull it into accounting software. The short answer to all of this is to keep track of all the money that comes in, the money that goes out, and having an idea as to when it is all going to happen.

On first pass, the cash flow will look a lot like your income statement. This example is going to show what cash flow looks like over a given year, and why it is important to understand when money is coming in and going out:

Sample Cash Flow

	Q1	Q2	Q3	Q4	Total for Year
Cash Flow from Operations					0
Net Income	3,450	7,750	9,050	(15,550)	4,700
Adjustments for depreciation					0
Adjustments for increase in inventories	2,500	(500)	(1,000)		1,000
Adjustments for decreases in accounts recievable					0
Net Cash Flow from Operations	5,950	7,250	8,050	(15,550)	5,700
Cash Flow from Investing					0
Cash receipts from use of property/equipment					0
Cash paid for purchase of equipment	(2,000)				(2,000)
Net Cash Flows from Investing	(2,000)	0	0	0	(2,000)
Cash Flows from Financing					
Loans taken out	4,500				4,500
Loan Payments	(500)	(750)	(750)	(750)	(2,750)
Net Cash Flow from Financing	4,000	(750)	(750)	(750)	1,750
Net Increase in Cash	7,950	6,500	7,300	(16,300)	5,450

Depending on your contracts, publishers, and methods of delivery, it can easily be sixty to ninety days, or even longer before the author is paid for books and other products sold. Even if your publisher pays an advance on royalties, these amounts are much smaller than in years past, and paid over two to three draws (signing of the contract, final delivery of the manuscript, publication and release). If you attend and sell books at events and conventions, you have to buy those books up front, cover expenses, and there are no guarantees on the sale of product.

As you mature into your writing career, you will learn the patterns and the ebb and flow of earnings from your work. Understanding these patterns allows you to plan and manage your business, and your personal financial needs. Cash flow over a long term is the number one tool to give you insight into your investments and their return.

Hanging in the Balance

For our author, we've gotten a look at the comings and goings of their money. But what is their business really worth?

The business' value down into three pieces:

- Assets - Assets are the parts of the business that have value and can be sold or traded. Some assets, like laptops, depreciate and are worth less over time.

- Liabilities - The debts you and your company owe are liabilities. They come in both short term, such as utilities and longer term like mortgage payments.

- Owner's Equity - Once you have deducted the liabilities from the assets, you are left with the actual value of the business.

Here's the balance sheet over the same year:

Sample Balance Sheet

Assets		Liablities	
Current Assets		Current Liabilities	
Cash	2,950	Accounts Payable	1,750
Accounts Recievable		Accrued Expenses	
Inventory	1,000	Unearned Revenue	27,500
Total Current Assets	3,950	Total Current Liabilities	29,250
		Long-term liabilities	0
Long Term Assets		Total Liabilities	29,250
Equipment	2,000		
Depreciation	0	Owners Equity	
Total Long Term Assets	2,000	Retained Earnings & OE	(23,300)
		Total Owner's Equity	
Total Assets	5,950	Total Liabilities and Owner's Equity	5,950

Notice anything? Our author owes $23,300 more than his business is worth despite the fact they are making money. How can that be? Their career is taking off.

There are a few tricks in the numbers:

- The largest liability is the unearned revenue tied to the books that have not yet "earned out."

- It may be that some of the revenues from this year are advances on royalties paid because the contract has been signed, or the manuscript delivered, but the book has not yet been published or has just gone on sale

- It could be the overall value placed on the books is wrong. Declaring an overall value of any particular title is somewhat subjective and based on the experience of the publisher. It is rarely correct, and many books never "earn out" their advance.

- In the example above, once a book has completely earned out, it doesn't mean that additional sales and future royalties can't come in, it just means the book is getting to the end of its projected life for the majority of its sales. It also means any potential liability from not having "earned out" has been satisfied. While there is still value in the title, it can be hard to estimate. If it becomes a runaway best seller, you may revalue the overall title from year to year. The same is true if it's a non-seller.
- Regardless, you carry the liability on the title not having earned out until either it finally reaches the advance, or the publisher returns rights to the author and ends the contract.

It is also worth remembering that the value of your business is not a reflection of your value as an author. Unlike most businesses, where the major assets are intellectual property being licensed, much of the actual value can look like a liability for the business. Depending on the contracts and agreements, it's very different carrying the liability for a book that hasn't earned out and owing for books (inventory) purchased on a credit card.

Retained Earnings

The retained earnings statement is simple compared to everything else. It is simply noting how much your business is worth this year compared to the previous one.

Sample Retained Earnings

Beginning Balance		
Retained Earnings as of January 1		0
Plus: Net Income		4,700
		4,700
Less: Owner Draws		28,000
Retained Earnings as of December 31:		(23,300)

Even as a sole proprietor, it is your business and your money, but you need to remember some of those resources are necessary to keep your business and career well fed and growing before you consider taking from it for yourself (your owner draws).

Budgets

All of us are familiar with budgets, at least the idea, even though most of us don't particularly like to do them. It's a necessary part of life. When we were talking about the plans, we touched on budgets somewhat, but now we're going to dive deeper into that pool.

For your individual budget, it probably looks something like this:

Monthly Budget:		
Monthly Income		
Description	*Amount*	
Bob's Job	2,250	
Jane's Job	2,250	
Total:		*4,500*
Monthly Expenses:		
Description	*Amount*	
Mortgage	1,000	
Truck Payment	600	
Car Payment	450	
School	350	
Food	800	
Insurance	200	
Entertainment	200	
Other	400	
Savings	500	
Total:		*4,500*

Your business and project budgets are going to work in much the same way, but the details will vary by project or business. Another big difference, your budget is going to focus first on expenses, so you know how much revenue you need to generate. You'll find there are differences between your budget for your business overall vs. a project budget.

Having a budget is valuable for several reasons:

- You have a picture of what revenues you need to generate to cover expenses.
- You plan for the resources a specific project will require to complete.
- You have targets to measure your actual business performance against.

- Comparing your actual results against your budget, you can illustrate what adjustments you need to make, and develop a better model to operate your business.

On an annual basis, you'll want to come up with your operational budget, planning for how much you'll spend each month. The reason being, you have some expenses that will happen occasionally such as buying a new computer, and others that are monthly or annual subscriptions.

In this example, (it's not based on our first set of financial statements, so you can see what something a little more complex looks like) I do the budget by quarters. In practice, I suggest doing it monthly.

Sample Budget

Revenues		Q1	Q2	Q3	Q4	Total
Project						
	Book 1 - physical	998	12,968	3,990	1,995	19,950
	Book 1 - ebook	5,240	17,465	6,986	5,240	34,930
	Book 1 - audiobook	14,049	46,831	18,732	14,049	93,662
	Book 2 - ebook		873	12,226	4,366	17,465
Total Revenues		**20,286**	**78,137**	**41,934**	**25,650**	**166,007**
Direct Expenses						
	Commissions	499	6,484	1,995	998	9,975
	Printing	305	3,965	1,220	610	6,100
	Shipping	49	631	194	97	970
	Editing	4,000	3,000			7,000
	Cover	800	500			1,300
Total Direct Expenses		*5,652*	*14,579*	*3,409*	*1,705*	*25,345*
Indirect Expenses						
	Website	1,000	1,000	1,000	1,000	4,000
	Marketing	1,500	7,000	1,000	500	10,000
Total Indirect Expenses		*2,500*	*8,000*	*2,000*	*1,500*	*14,000*
Total Expenses		**8,152**	**22,579**	**5,409**	**3,205**	**39,345**
Pre-tax Income		12,134	55,558	36,525	22,446	126,662
Estimated Federal Tax		3,034				
Estimated State Tax		728				
Net Income		*8,373*	*55,558*	*36,525*	*22,446*	*126,662*

While this is a simple budget (and it ties to your COGS example) you can see the revenues and expenses from each of your individual projects, and your overhead. The assumptions are that you paid for your editing and cover expenses in Q1 just before the book launch, and that the expenses for book 2 were paid just before it launched at the end of Q2.

When doing your budgets and estimations, expect for your books to have a longer tail, but most of your sales will happen closer to the launch.

As you go through the year, compare your actual efforts, expenditures and revenues against your budget. Not only does it give you a benchmark to know how you're performing, it also will help you improve your estimation process for the future. If necessary, adjust the budget through the year.

The Value of Time (Your Most Precious Resource)

"My favorite things in life don't cost any money. It's really clear that the most precious resource we all have is time."
— *Steve Jobs*

So far, we've been talking finances. There is another critical resource you need to budget and spend even more wisely: your time.

Time is finite, and the only way to make more is to hire out for some work to be done.

As a business owner, you should understand where your time goes, and the returns. It's one thing to come up with financial projections, but how do you break down your time, and understand the investment for the return?

Based on an average forty-hour week, that's 2080 hours a year if you never take a vacation. Let's call it 2000 working hours a year.

I challenge you to keep a diary of where you spend your time, or if you're brave, load tools on your computer and smartphone to keep you honest. If you looked at an eight-hour day, where did your time go? Was it writing? Marketing? Surfing social media for cat videos and calling it engagement?

All of us suffer from procrastination or wasting time we call productive, when we are just keeping busy. Improving your time management, especially your creative time, is an easy way to get more done, especially those tasks that we hate but must be completed.

On you have gathered some actual numbers about how and where you spend your time, categorize it as:

- Project specific, by project
- Overhead, such as marketing or accounting
- Other (a nice way of saying you were looking at cat videos and aren't trying to call it part of your marketing time)

Let's say you spend 20 hours a week over eight weeks total to draft, edit, and get a book out the door. 160 hours total. It can even be spread over a year. Now assume over the first year of that book's life it sells 1,000 ebooks, and your net income on each is $2.00 (assuming this is after all of the direct expenses of the book). This means you've earned $2,000, or $12.50 an hour. What if you can spend an extra 5 hours a week (1 hour a day) on marketing for three months, and that pushes your sales to 1500 copies. Now you have 225 hours into a book for $3,000 in sales, or $13.33 an hour. Another way to look at it, if you budgeted based on 1,000 books sold, and hit that target, you worked 65 hours to make $1,000, or $15.38 an hour.

Now consider your overhead. It keeps spending whether you are writing, marketing, or looking at cat videos.

I'm not saying work 100 hours a week. I've done it a lot in my life, and I can't recommend it. My point is *value* your time. It's yours to spend however you want, and if you want a successful business and career, make the most of the time you set aside to work.

Now take this method and use it to compare your other projects. Make a grid that lists the projects and their effective hourly rates:

Sample Time Budget

Project	Hours to bring to market	Hours Marketing	Revenues	Effective Rate
Book 1	160.00	65.00	3,000.00	13.33
Short Story1	5.00		100.00	20.00
Short Story 2	10.00		150.00	15.00
Article	1.00		50.00	50.00

Look at the effective hourly rate by project. The net revenue shouldn't be your only factor in doing the work. Yes, the article got you $50 an hour, and maybe you want to cultivate doing more of those, but you only get paid once. The short stories make a good rate compared to the book, but how much work does it take to sell them? And over time, short stories and novels will continue to generate revenues where articles typically do not.

Maybe it's the articles you publish that get you steady work while you build your career. Or it could be the book that gets you the copywriting jobs for articles. I'm not telling you what decision to make, I'm only giving you tools to use in the decision-making process. Your revenue streams and where you spend your time depend on you and your goals.

One important difference to consider here is that you are not calculating a figure here to decide what you pay yourself. It's not like having a job and working an extra shift will pay a fixed hourly rate. You are calculating it to determine how well the time you spend of time produces a return on the investment. It shouldn't dictate the projects you take but should be a consideration.

I'm including a blog post I wrote years ago about the cost of doing the author business and dealing with customers. I hadn't re-read it in years, and debated including it, but all authors have felt this at some point. Every person I know who has tried to run their own business has felt this at some time. So, overlook the bitter tang and know it will happen to you too. When it does, don't let it affect your relationship with future readers.

The Stark Economics (2015)

Once again, the cycle has come around, and it's come in full force. It's about supporting your favorite authors, buying their stuff and not stealing it.

First, let me say, I believe the vast majority of people are good and well-intentioned, but it only takes a very few people to convince you the world needs a good cleansing zombie apocalypse.

I did a sci-fi convention a couple of weeks back, and had a table talking about my books, and even had sold a few. A girl in her late twenties walked over to the table and asked for one of the scattered candy bars on my table, and I told her to help herself. She did.

She wanted to know about the books and we talked for about fifteen minutes, in that time she ate every one of the candy bars on my table (about 10) and then not so politely told me I needed to give her a free book because she couldn't afford it. Not even the ebooks, but a signed paperback. I politely declined, she told me to "F#$! off then" and left the pile of candy bar wrappers on my table.

I tossed the wrappers, had a small internal meltdown while keeping my exterior smile, wrote a few notes about how this self-entitled whiny %!@# is going to wind up dying in a future book, and moved on. Never piss off a writer with a twisted sense of humor, Miss-going-to-die-by- starving-to-death-while-being-dipped-into-a-vat-of-molten-chocolate, allowing it to harden, and watching you starve to death while ants eat the chocolate away. #RantOver #SanitizedVersion

At the same time, a very lovely young lady came to my table several times, a fellow writer, and we talked a lot through the weekend. She bought my ebook, and I gave her a print copy so she'd have a signed one.

We now live in a world of open source, where so many people think everything should be free, especially digital content. At a convention a while back, I had someone argue about why I was charging for books. Especially ebooks, because they don't cost anything.

So, let's break down the numbers:
Let's assume I'm a traditionally published author.
My percentage of sales will be 7 – 15%. Let's assume a blended rate of $4.99 a book between ebooks and print (Low by today's trade pub standards, but roll with me over the life of the book). Based on this, the author will make $0.35 to $0.75 a book. I'm feeling optimistic, so let's take $0.75 a book.

An average novel is 80,000 words. We won't talk about my last two novels in the 105k range. What does it take to crank out that 80,000 words?

A productive average is 1000 words an hour to draft, so that's 80 hours.

But wait, that's once you have an idea, research, flesh it out, plan, pitch and sell it. 80 hours. (And that's fiction. The reality is hundreds of hours or more.)

Depending on your style and productivity, editing, rewrites, and stuff that just didn't work? I've seen people estimate as little as another thirty to fifty percent of the original draft, but for a commercially published work, it's easily equal to four or five times the original first draft for the author to review edits, do rewrites, proofread, punctuation, and everything else. Not to mention the editors from the publishing house side. Let's split the difference, and call it 300 hours.

Arguing with editors, agents, cover artists, and other administrative crap? 40 hours.

So doing a little math, that's 500 hours. Based on 40-hour weeks, that's 12.5 weeks, so let's cut it to three months of working time, for 80,000 words.

Based on the proposed move to go to $15 an hour, and hopefully you think creative work is worth at least that, you have to sell... hmmmm carry the one, it's $7,500, and at $0.75 a copy, you need to sell 10,000 books. Let's say you sell 100 a week, and so that's two years of sales.

Not to mention the hours of marketing, social media, and cultivating your fan base that aren't in there.

But wait, there's more!

Let's say you're doing a self-published work.

Our productive average is 1000 words an hour to draft, so we'll still go with 80 hours.

But wait, you still have all of the other work your publisher would handle? You're on the hook for it now. Editing, rewrites, etc., and I'm going to assume you hire someone to edit, so you're still at the same 300 hours.

Arguing with editors, cover artists, and other administrative crap? I'll be generous and say add another 100 hours. So, doing a little math, that's 560 hours. Based on 40-hour weeks, that's 14 weeks, for 80,000 words.

Plus you have to pay for cover art - $100 - $250 (minimum) to thousands.

Editing will cost another $1,000 - $5,000 or more depending on the types of editing and level of polish you want to put on it. Or you have to put in the hours. And trust me, you need to have an external editor. Either way, you're spending the time and money.

I'm going to use an even $1,000 to produce the work (on the low end of what you should budget).

Depending on how you publish as exclusive or wide, Amazon is going to give you 35% - 70% of your sales. The down side, you probably are maxing out at $4.99, but we'll stick with it for equivalency. That's $1.75 to $3.50 a book from your distributor. We're rolling in the cash now!

You've laid out $1000 up front. So you need to sell 286 books to pay for that.

To sell those, you're looking at advertising, and getting reviews, another $1000. Another 286 books.

So just to cover my outlay, I need to sell 582 books. Wait, I forgot about the cover for $300, tack on another 143 books. We're up to 725 books to break even on my investment. At that point, I haven't made a dime. This also does not include the cost of attending conventions, renting booths, etc.

Show me the money!

At $3.50 a book to get minimum wage for my 560 hours, I need to sell another 2400 books! We're up to 3,125 books.

Most producing self-published authors average 5-50 sales a week. Let's say you are rocking it and doing 50 a week. That means I only need 63 weeks... at the same high pace to make my $15 an hour. Oh wait, now I don't have a publisher, or anyone else to help promote me. And most self-published would be happy at 5 a week after a couple of weeks. Most books retail at $2.99 meaning the author is looking at around two dollars a book. You're looking at 3-4 years, unless you push really hard, do a lot of advertising, and get a little lucky. And no book sells for that long unless there are follow up titles in the series to keep sales going.

Let's talk other opportunity costs. I work a full-time gig. Much of my life, it's been 60, 70, 80 hours a week. I do all of this at lunch and night when everyone else is asleep. Weekends. I'm behind on TV and movies. Most of what I read is research or stuff for fellow authors and friends.

So yeah, oh little Miss-self-important-snowflake-who-is-willing-to-drop-$5-on-a-latte-and-come-over-and-lecture-me-why-you-can't-spend-a- couple-of-bucks-for-an-ebook, and tell me it doesn't cost anything?

#RantOver

Time Management

Now that you can start to put a dollar figure to the time you spend on your business, you should think about how to manage your time to get a better return on investment. What if you can write more books or articles? Do more productive marketing? What if you can cut the 160 hours to bring a book to market to 120?

What is the value of those extra hours? A whole week's working time!

You can't swing a mouse click on Amazon without hitting something about productivity, be it work harder, work faster, or master the four-hour work week. I am not a master of productivity myself and wind up being the biggest offender of some of what I'm going to outline. I don't have a magic answer. There isn't one.

But I'm going to give you a few tools that work:

- Have an actual goal and create a roadmap to get you there. For every book and your career. You want to be a New York Times best-selling author? The most sought-after copywriter? Write a trilogy? Create a written plan.

  How do I create such a plan you ask? Break it down into bite sized chunks that are achievable. Need to deliver an eighty-thousand-word manuscript in thirty days? Easy. You need to hit four thousand words a day, Monday through Friday. Need to learn a new style guide? Lay out a study plan.

- Always be learning.

- Learn to prioritize. Not everything is equally important. Not everything will give you the same return. (And for one I haven't learned, make sure you are a priority too. Take some time for yourself and the family. Mind and body need a break sometime.)

- Have an accountability partner. Someone who you can bounce ideas off of, and who will also give you that reality check when you need it. Do the same for them.

- Admit when you suck at something. Learn to ask for help. Know when you need to hire something out.

- Be honest with yourself when you're procrastinating. "I don't have time" is 100% of the time an excuse. If it's a priority, you'll make time. If it's just something you're avoiding for whatever reason, own up to that. If you want to sit and vegetate in front of the TV, do it. Just don't feel guilty or complain later.

- Get some exercise. And some sleep. I'm guilty on these counts.

- Work on getting a little better every day. Here's a secret…if you do something every day, you will get better. Or at least suck less.

- Start with the thing you want to do least. As Mark Twain said, *"If it's your job to eat a frog, it's best to do it first thing in the morning. And if it's your job to eat two frogs, it's best to eat the biggest one first."*

- Sit down and start. It's easier to fix something than to look at the blank page. This should be number one, but it's here for emphasis.

I'm going to add one more here, because it's a frequent problem for me, and it's one my editors (rightly) told me I'd ignored in this list. Know when you are overcommitted, and then prioritize. I'm usually very aware when I do it. Sometimes, life just happens and blows up the best laid plans. When it happens, and it will, don't spend time stressing over it, reprioritize. Sometimes that means deciding to delay or cut what you want to do vs. what you need to do.

Freelancing Doesn't Mean Free

Ever paid your rent with exposure? How about bought a car? Gone to a movie? Gotten a cup of coffee to keep your creative juices flowing at two a.m.?

No? Try tipping the delivery guy with exposure.

We are often asked to put our creative talents to use for others. Every creative person has been asked to do free work for the "exposure." Most of us have even done it at one time or another.

People die from exposure. It's one way of getting attention, but no one that will help your business.

It could be as simple as drafting copy for a press release for a charity function or complex as doing cover art for an event. Maybe it's drafting a story for an anthology.

But this can also be much more than a small effort.

Maybe you cut your rates to write a piece to get into a larger publisher, or with someone where you are looking to build a connection. Or worst, you contract to do a piece of work, and the other party simply doesn't pay on delivery.

I'm not suggesting not to do it. When you choose to do these things, you are doing it because you want to, or to support the cause, not for some other never-to-be realized "exposure" benefit.

I have cut my rates from time-to-time to help someone out, or knowing they would make it right on a later job, but it takes a tight relationship or was something I believed in.

It's easy for people to overlook the work and value in creative outlets. It can also be easy, if not deliberate, for some to discount the product of creative efforts, and take advantage of your work.

It is up to you, as the producer and business owner, to ensure this doesn't happen to you.

- It is important, no, critical for you to place value on your own work. See and know it's worth. Don't be afraid to demand to be compensated appropriately for it.
- Do the same for others. Respect and value their work as well.
- Always have a contract, even if you are working for "exposure."
- Be ready to enforce the contract.
- Never work for free. If you elect to donate your work for a cause, look at it that way, A donation of your talents, skills, and craft. If some benefit comes of it, all the better.

Value yourself and your skills. Make sure others value it as well.

Too Good to be True

The old adage holds as true in business as it does in life; if it sounds too good to be true, it probably is. In the age of the internet, we all have seen spam and ads promising the earth, moon and stars for one low, low price. But wait, there's more!

We have all been in a position where we've gotten impatient, and even desperate to make something happen. The words won't flow with a deadline approaching, or the air conditioner dies when it's a hundred degrees outside. Suddenly you spot that perfect ad, or someone introduces you to the ideal person that can fix all your problems.

For a price.

I'm one of those people who gets paid to fix problems and improve performance. Advertising is part of any business. I've worked with and for one-person start-ups and Fortune 50 companies. I'm selective about the clients I take on and won't take money from someone I don't believe I can materially help.

I also don't promise things I don't have a track record of delivering.

There's a lot of people out there who can't say the same thing.

As a small business, you can't do it all, and certainly not effectively. None of us know everything, so how do we go about deciding if a product, service or partner is for us, and if it's worth the cost?

It all boils down to *caveat emptor*. May the buyer beware.

Admittedly, I try a lot of products and services. Sometimes it's for an article or review, sometimes it's to fill a need. And sometimes it's just curiosity. Here are some guidelines I suggest using to evaluate investment in your business:

- Do I have an actual gap or need the product fills, or is it something else to sit unused?
- Do I know anyone that's tried or used it? Recommended it?
- What do the reviews and feedback say online?
- Is there a free trial?
- What's the return policy?
- Is the cost of the product or service commensurate with the benefit to you?
- Are the costs in line with similar products or services in the market?
- If the product or service doesn't deliver what you need, can you absorb the cost?

Let me give you an example. Most small and medium sized businesses have at least evaluated, if not used a product called Infusionsoft, designed as a sales, marketing, email list, and customer data management system. It works very well for a lot of uses but can be overkill for small businesses. And it starts at several hundred dollars a month.

If you're doing thousands, tens of thousands or more in eCommerce sales a month, it usually makes sense. If you have a small reader base and are just looking to send out a newsletter, there are much more cost-effective ways of getting the same result.

The same goes with people promising writing or publishing services. Vanity presses, at one time, were the main avenue for the self-published. They still hold sway for those who want to go out under a publisher's label but haven't been able to secure a traditional publisher. (Note: no matter what they call themselves, they aren't publishers. They are services companies. Or outright scams.) As a general rule, these services bundle products and services needed to bring a book to market but can be expensive in comparison to managing the covers, editing, etc. yourself. You will also find that many have large numbers of complaints about over-committing and under-delivering on their services, and requiring authors pay hefty sums to the production of their book (remember Yog's law.)

I say this not to scare you or warn you away. I simply encourage you to not make snap decisions and take the time to do your homework, no matter how much you want to rush your book to print.

Wrapping it up

What's next?

As long as you keep going, you'll keep getting better. And as you get better, you gain more confidence. That alone is success.
- Tamara Taylor

I started this book talking about the Tesla and Edison wars. Why did I do that? I haven't really come back to them. The stories of both men, as have many others, have been inspirations, and taught me lessons in my life.

Nikolai Tesla was a brilliant man who, even at his peak, had a small lab and staff, yet he created the basis for our modern world. He was driven to do it not for profit but for the betterment of all mankind.

Thomas Edison was also a genius. Not only was he an inventor and innovator, he was a ruthless and driven businessman. He knew how to find the best minds and build a team. His companies created much of the modern industrial world in which we live.

I've worked with scientists, engineers, developers, and some great business minds in my career. I often hear people from both sides lament that if the pair had only worked together, how much more they could have accomplished. In an ideal world, I would agree.

But we do not live in an ideal world.

I argue that part of the success of both men came from their rivalry; their desire to outperform the other. They each had spies reporting back from each other's labs, and often took different approaches to solving the same needs and challenges. It was an age of pioneers with few rules, and in that setting two men took extremely different views, and their competition created our modern world.

Business is changing. The world now thrives from collaboration and partnership. We're in a revival period of entrepreneurship and creativity.

I was raised in small business and, so far, have had a successful career consulting in a number of industries, and working with some amazing technologies. I've also had the good fortune to write and bring some of my ideas to life.

I started Author Essentials (https://www.authoressentials.net), of which this book is a part, in an effort to help fellow creative people survive and thrive in a competitive and often self-destructive business. We're often our own worst enemies when it comes to profiting from our work.

This book is only part of what is planned for Author Essentials, and while there is a lot here, it's only the very basic level of operating a business. Many pieces hit the cutting room floor. Some of those have become articles on the site or will in the future. Others may wind up in subsequent books and modules.

I hope you have gained something from this work, and it helps get you to the next level of success. I want to hear from you. I want to know if this book helped and what could be better. What questions you have, and most of all, celebrate your successes large and small.

To quote the great Freddie Mercury: "Get on your bike and ride."

- Jim

Bonuses and Additional Resources

FB Group

About the Author

James Nettles has consulted on and managed business and technological transformation projects in North and South America, Europe and Asia for businesses from startups to Fortune 100's, and about everything in between.

He is a University of South Carolina graduate in Entrepreneurial Management and Management Information Systems, with studies in Anthropology, Sociology and Philosophy. A fiction and nonfiction author, he got his start in media in college, and continues to write, speak and consult in the fields of privacy, artificial and business intelligence, next generation technologies, business process and strategy, and entrepreneurship as well as writing tools, technology, and craft.

He currently lives in Charlotte, NC with his wife and hounds.

He is the CEO and founding partner for Author Essentials, a project started by writers, for writers.

He can be reached at:
Email: jimn@authoressentials.net
Facebook: **https://www.facebook.com/jimmacauthor**
Twitter: @jimmacauth

Every business is a writing business

52865917R00135

Made in the USA
Columbia, SC
12 March 2019